Dr Ruth Hie King WONG was at

Harvard University from 1962-1963

where she did her Ed M and EdD.

She was the first Director of the

National Institute of Education, Singapore (1973-1976)

and hailed as a trail blazer in education for Singapore.

With Compliments from

Professor Oon-Seng TAN

Director of the National Institute of Education, Singapore (2014-2018)

Yidan Visiting Global Fellow

Harvard Graduate School of Education

Global Voices in Education

Oon Seng Tan · Hee Ong Wong
Seok Hoon Seng
Editors

Global Voices in Education

Ruth Wong Memorial Lectures, Volume II

 Springer

Editors
Oon Seng Tan
National Institute of Education
Singapore
Singapore

Seok Hoon Seng
Singapore
Singapore

Hee Ong Wong
Singapore
Singapore

ISBN 978-981-10-3538-8   ISBN 978-981-10-3539-5   (eBook)
DOI 10.1007/978-981-10-3539-5

Library of Congress Control Number: 2016961331

Cover photo from Ruth Wong: Educationist and Teacher Extraordinaire, 2013, with permission from Strategic Information and Research Development Centre.

Printed on acid-free paper

This Springer imprint is published by Springer Nature
The registered company is Springer Nature Singapore Pte Ltd.
The registered company address is: 152 Beach Road, #22-06/08 Gateway East, Singapore 189721, Singapore

Preface

This book, together with the previous published volume (Tan et al. 2015) form a complete compilation of the annual Ruth Wong memorial lectures from 1983 to 2008. The chronological order in which the lectures were given is recorded in the Appendix.

Ruth Wong Hie King 1918–1982 (Ruth Wong: educationist and teacher extraordinaire, 2013, with permission from Strategic Information and Research Development Centre)

The decision to compile the lectures for publication as a memoir for posterity took root with the discovery of transcripts left behind by the late Dr. Wong Poi Kwong, brother of Ruth Wong. These transcripts were those of the Memorial Lectures instituted to commemorate the missionary zeal and rich legacy left by the founding Director of the Institute of Education, Dr. Ruth Wong, a trail blazer in the field of education (Wong 2013). Internationally renowned professors and leading experts in education were invited as orators. The educational themes dealt with in these lectures were that on teaching and learning, children and learning and education as a profession. They represent the many ways Ruth's vision, ideas and innovation elevated the training and education of teachers, and improved the learning experiences and education of children in Singapore's journey to a world class education system.

In compiling these lectures the first difficulty encountered was to trace the missing transcripts. After many attempts and great patience, Dr. Seng Seok Hoon, the chief organizer of the lectures was contacted. We soon discovered that the transcripts were kept in one of 40 boxes! Although help was at hand to open the boxes one by one; by divine guidance the fifth box she opened, much to our delight, contained majority of the transcripts. However, miraculously (one was discovered in a library and another fell out from a dust laden cover) we were able to trace all. It was with much faith that this task was undertaken to its completion—the search for original transcripts, contacting the speakers for permission to publish, the choice of publisher, the permission for reproduction from publishers, and the editing of scripts. The synopsis of Julian Elliott's lecture was compiled from a slide presentation.

It is amazing how the three co-editors came together each time to reflect on the influence of Dr. Ruth Wong. We actually span some two generations. Hee Ong is Ruth's sister whom she impacted as a family member, role model and mentor. Seok Hoon was Ruth's protégé and associate. Oon Seng was a teenager and undergraduate who was deeply inspired by Dr. Ruth Wong's philosophy of life and call. Despite all our tight schedules, there was much enthusiasm and passion amongst us for the simple reason that we have been touched by the faith, vision and commitment of Dr. Ruth Wong and the fruits of her labour for education and humanity.

For Prof. Tan Oon Seng, Director of National Institute of Education (NIE), Dr. Ruth Wong's work continues to influence teacher education till this day. The seeds of her ideals see fruition at NIE in the influence of preparing all teachers and school leaders in Singapore. NIE's teacher education has been a global influence today in terms of policies, programmes, practices and research in education. In his first and several investitures of graduating cohorts of teachers, Prof. Tan repeatedly mentioned and quoted Dr. Ruth Wong to illustrate the call and care of the teacher. In the Foreword of *Ruth Wong: Educationist and Teacher Extraordinaire*, Prof. Tan wrote that one key lesson he learned from Ruth was that "God has a calling for each of us in a vocation where He will make us a blessing to others" (Tan 2013, p. xi). He recalled vividly how Dr. Ruth Wong exclaimed the day he told her he was going into teaching: "Wow, you are going to be a teacher... and a math teacher" (Tan 2013, p. xii). And how in that one afternoon she shared passionately what it meant to be a true educator with the love and concern for the children of generations to come. Dr. Ruth Wong indeed sowed the seeds of almost all the important aspects of education from the holistic care for the learner and preparing teachers grounded in values and competencies to building teacher education informed by research and investing in every child in education.

Seok Hoon was Oon Seng's teacher and mentor when he was pursuing his Master and Ph.D. studies. Their professional relationship reflect very much the relationship between Seok Hoon and her mentor Dr. Ruth Wong. Both mentor and mentee understand how important this link is between the teacher and the learner. Seok Hoon's professional career was very much influenced by Dr. Ruth Wong's foresight in her quest to improve the academic standing of the academic staff in NIE; under her tutelage and guidance, many NIE staff were sent overseas for doctoral studies.

Educators, education leaders and policy makers interested in uplifting and flourishing education for their next generation of learners reading these two volumes, should feel the inspiration, as well as find benefit and challenges from the experiences of global renowned educators.

The editors are also delighted to share that all the royalties of this volume will go to fund the Ruth Wong Professorship inaugurated in June 2015.

Singapore   Oon Seng Tan
                                                                                           Hee Ong Wong
                                                                                           Seok Hoon Seng

References

Tan, O. S. (2013). Foreword. In H. O. Wong (Ed.), *Ruth Wong: Educationist and teacher extraordinaire* (pp. xi–xiii). Petaling Jaya, Malaysia: Strategic Information and Research Development Centre.

Tan, O. S., Wong, H. O., & Seng, S. H. (Eds.). (2015). *Global voices in education: Ruth Wong memorial lectures*. Singapore: Springer.

Wong, H. O. (2013). *Ruth Wong: Educationist and teacher extraordinaire*. Petaling Jaya, Malaysia: Strategic Information and Research Development Centre.

Acknowledgements

Global Voices in Education: Ruth Wong Memorial Lectures, Volume II bears the imprint of many individuals who have come to appreciate the legacy of Dr. Ruth Wong. Our thanks to all our distinguished speakers: Marie M. Clay, Ungku Abdul Aziz, Lucrecia R. Kasilag, Gungwu Wang, Awang Had Salleh, Paul Min Phang Chang, Jasbir Kaur, Hon Chan Chai, Warwick Elley and Julian Elliott.

Our thanks to the organizing team for the memorial lectures especially Dr. Ho Wah Kam (a close colleague of Ruth Wong, whose personal contact with the speakers brought them from foreign shores to contribute their voices in education), Dr. Seng Seok Hoon and the late Dr. Wong Poi Kwong, brother of Ruth Wong.

We would also like to thank Mrs. Wan-Yeoh Seok Kwan, Head of NIE Library for superbly co-ordinating this project and her staff especially Ow Tsin Li Stephanie.

A special thanks to Mr. Paradijs van Harmen, Mr. Lawrence Liu and the great editorial team from Springer.

Our acknowledgement and thanks to the National Institute of Education, Singapore for permission to reproduce copyright material pertaining to the *Singapore Journal of Education* (now known as *Asia Pacific Journal of Education*).

Our acknowledgement and thanks to Taylor & Francis and Springer for permission to reproduce copyright material.

Our acknowledgement and thanks to the Strategic Information and Research Development Centre for permission to reproduce copyright material.

Contents

Chapter 1
Beginning Literacy in Two Languages

Marie Mildred Clay

In many parts of the world bilingual situations present unsolved problems for education and for the teaching of reading and writing in particular. All questions we have about literacy instruction are raised to another level of complexity when children are faced with learning their mother tongue and one, or even two, more languages. However when a society is clear about its language policies then the problems of teaching children to read in the mother tongue and in another language can be faced and solutions worked out.

The most consistent advice available in the literature today is for parents of a language group to use their own language with their preschool children so that they enter school with good control of their first language. This provides a sound foundation for education. Of course schools then have some consequential challenges to face. The second recommendation commonly implemented today is to have children learn to read in their mother tongue while they are learning to speak the second language. They begin to read that second language after a year or two. This recommendation may be incompatible with the complex language situation you have here in Singapore and serves to point out clearly that every language situation is different. There are no ready-made solutions to the particular language situations that are found in different societies. As I understand it you have a good record of funding research which asks questions about what works well in your schools. As there is no overseas expert who can bring you the essential solution to Singaporean questions, you have to problem-solve to find the solutions for your schools. From the outside we can only suggest options.

Marie Mildred Clay (Dame Commander of the Order of the British Empire)—Passed away.

M.M. Clay (✉)
Wellington, New Zealand

© Springer Nature Singapore Pte Ltd. 2017
O.S. Tan et al. (eds.), *Global Voices in Education*,
DOI 10.1007/978-981-10-3539-5_1

The two themes of my remarks today will be that children need to hear and use the languages they are learning to read and write and secondly that we should enlist the power-to-learn that children bring to school and let them relate what they already know to our lessons. We should not destroy the wholeness of the real understanding that young children have about the world they live in by an unnecessary emphasis on detail, on correctness, on separate bits of knowledge or skill which they cannot relate to anything they already know. In speaking of these points I will refer to some emphases in research today by illustration rather than reporting the research itself.

I will assume throughout my talk that you have established reading, writing and oral language programmes. I will try to persuade you to include in those programmes activities which you may not yet include. For this you may have to borrow time from other activities but you would not necessarily give those established practices up. The activities I will discuss apply to children learning to read and write

in   their mother tongue
or   another language
or   even in two languages at once.

Three Bilingual Children—Illustrative Cases

Eruera Stirling, A New Zealand Maori

To set the scene let me take you back to the childhood of an eminent Maori elder who recently died in my home city of Auckland at the age of 80 years. He had a Maori mother and a European father, and, as was the custom, he was sent to live with his grandparents for most of his preschool years. He related his autobiography to Anne Salmond, an anthropologist, who was taking down an oral history of his life.

> When I arrived at the home of my father and mother, I wasn't happy with the pakeha (white man's) way. Our father was (a white man) a builder and he had built a big home for us with a piano and everything, but I missed our little nikau hut in the bush. I couldn't speak any English, and when my father spoke English to my brothers, I didn't know what he was saying. Every time he spoke to me, my brothers had to tell me what he wanted …

> The first day I went to school at Raukikore, I wasn't interested in the other children and their games. I walked away from school into the paddocks and I was talking to the seagulls and the sparrows in Maori. Those were the sounds of my young days, the singing of the birds and the noises of the bush. In those days though, if anybody was found speaking the Maori language at school they'd get a hiding for it, and on my first day at school I was taken inside and the teacher gave me a warning. I didn't know what he was talking about so they had to get my brother Tai, and Tai told me not to talk Maori at school any more. The trouble was, I couldn't speak anything else and school life was not very happy for me at the start. I kept away from the other children, I wasn't interested in playmates and I got worse and worse, my mind kept going back to that other life and I didn't like school – I was more

interested in the past. Pretty nearly every day I'd get a hiding, and one morning I got so wild I refused to come into the classroom, I stayed outside talking Maori to the birds. They had to come and get me, and the master gave me a very strong thrashing. The marks showed on my hands and feet, and I cried and cried and cried!

When I arrived home my mother … cried too. My father … looked at the marks on my hands and feet and he was wild. He said to Mum, 'I am not going to work tomorrow, I'm going to see that headmaster!'

The next morning Dad took me to school, and when the bell rang Dad went over to Mr. Mulhern, the headmaster. 'Don't you ever give my son the strap again, you bloody Irishman! If you touch him again I'll give you a hiding – you leave him alone!'

They had a few words about it but after a while they calmed down, and Dad said, 'This son of mine is the only one in the whole school who has been through the channel with the old people, in the real Maori way. You've got to give him time to pick up, I don't want you to punish him again; their way is different and you have to help him and be good to him …

The next day when I went to school, Mr. Mulhern's daughter Kathleen came to me and took me away, we had a little room to ourselves and she started to give me special lessons. I didn't like her at first, but she kept on with it and gave me a pencil, and started to point out the writing to me, and in the end I listened to her. She taught me the a b c at our little table and she was nice. Within a few weeks I was really interested in schoolwork, and when I went home after school I'd get out my books and sit in the corner of our house and study …

I kept on with school … and when they had the test at school, they found I was progressing quicker than the other children … I had this belief that my work with the old people was helping me with my studies, and when we started reading our books on Maori history, I looked at those histories and I thought, I've got a more important history behind me than anything written in these books. (Stirling 1980, pp. 94–95)

That extract makes me think of languages and beginning school and the problem of understanding what is going on in the classroom. I am impressed with the sense of being educated and the feeling of power over language that Eruera remembered from his youth.

Richard Rodriguez, A Spanish-American

Let me take another example, this time a Spanish-speaking child trying to learn to read in English. It comes from an autobiography called *Hunger of Memory*.

I needed to look up whole paragraphs of words in a dictionary. Lines of type were dizzying, the eye having to move slowly across the page, then down, and across … The sentence of the first books I read were coolly impersonal. Toned hard. What most bothered me, however, was the isolation reading required. To console myself for the loneliness I'd feel when I read, I tried reading in a very soft voice. Until: 'Who is doing all that talking to his neighbour?' Shortly after, remedial reading classes were arranged for me with a very old nun.

At the end of each school day, for nearly six months, I would meet with her in the tiny room that served as the school's library but was actually only a storeroom for used textbooks and a vast collection of *National Geographics*. Everything about our sessions pleased me: the smallness of the room; the noise of the janitor's broom hitting the edge of the long hallway outside the door; the green of the sun, lighting the wall; and the old woman's face blurred white with a beard. Most of the time we took turns; I began with my elementary text. Sentences of astonishing simplicity seemed to me lifeless and drab: 'The boys ran from the rain … She wanted to sing … The kite rose in the blue.' Then the old nun would read from *her* favorite books, usually biographies of early American presidents. Playfully she ran through complex sentences calling the words alive with her voice, making it seem that the author somehow was speaking directly to me. I smiled just to listen to her. I sat there and sensed for the very first time some possibility of fellowship between a reader and writer…

One day the nun concluded a session by asking me why I was so reluctant to read by myself. I tried to explain; said something about the way written words made me feel all alone … as if I spoke to myself in a room just emptied of furniture … she replied that I had nothing to fear. Didn't I realize that reading would open up whole new worlds? A book could open doors for me … I listened with respect. But her words were not influential. I was thinking then of another consequence of literacy, one I was too shy to admit but nonetheless trusted. Books were going to make me educated. That confidence enabled me, several months later, to overcome my fear of the silence. (Rodriguez 1982, pp. 63–65)

Both Rodriguez and Stirling learned a great deal from teachers who gave them individual teaching at school but only a few bilingual children can have those opportunities. It might be interesting for teachers in bilingual programmes and particularly for teachers-in-training to read biographies of bilingual childhoods. Perhaps students in training would find the taking of oral histories about learning to be literate a sensitising experience.

Now to my favourite five year old story-teller. Tomai's parents came from the Cook Islands in the South Pacific. They probably spoke the Cook Island language at home. He had been at school for six weeks. Tomai was invited by a Radio N. Z. interviewer to retell the story of *Goldilocks and The Three Bears*. Just prior to this in his classroom a child had been reprimanded by the teacher for playing with the electric plugs and suitable explanations and warnings had been given. He asked the interviewer if he could tell 'another story'. Wisely she agreed. Listen for this 5 year old's cautionary tale and his attempt to talk about something like artificial respiration and the application of oxygen. At the end of the story he brings the victim back to life and sets him up like new.

A Cautionary Tale

One day there was a little boy and there was a muvva. And so Muvva was gone shopping. And brother he saw a little … um a light came on. And so he broked it and he so he put his hands in the thing and he died and he shaked and he died. And Mum come home from shopping and as she looked for him and she said 'Oh! My God! He is died. I'd better ring up the police'. So she rang up the police. And so- the mans came. And so they got him. And – they've got a fing to carry him and they put him.. and they … and they put the things in. And and they put him in the um the hospital and they <u>do</u> it. And and he wasn't still up and they and they push his leg, *squeeze* him, squash him, and and and he open his eyes like vis and he shaked'd again and died. An' you know what? He… his mother came. And and the little boy waked up and they'd made his hands nice. And they – just cut his hands off. And they put a new hands on – and they put – cut his head off and they put a new head on and – cut his leg off and they put another leg on. And then cut in another leg and they put it on and and and he was up and when they finished and and and they've got some fings to put in his mouth – some drink of water and sugar in his in his little thing and he drinked it and the Muvva gave him some milk and he sucked it and he waked up.

Obviously Tomai has a good sense of story. The urge to tell that story breaks through all the barriers of his limited control over language. There is a wholeness to the encounter—a five year old on the way to becoming a more competent five year old. His language, his ideas, his level of thinking, his limitations of expression, but most of all his strengths come together in this creative outpouring of what he understood the teacher to say. Where did he get the art of the storyteller?

Little children think differently from adults and yet they manage to talk to those adults quite well, and in those conversations they develop their home language and their understanding of the immediate world around them. Developmentally the network of connections is from the child, through his family experiences and his mother tongue to the world of school where he may encounter another language, the language of the teacher and of the curriculum.

Actively Connecting with the School

It is well accepted in child development today that the child's psychological growth is the product of his active attempts to make sense of his own experience (Kagan 1971). The child is not passively moulded by his environment. Tomai could tell stories but (as we shall see later) he could not tell the story of Goldilocks and the Three Bears in the language of the book. He could tell it very well in his own English words. All children have active ways of making sense of the world of school when they first encounter it. To think about their new experiences children use the images from their past and they try actively to make sense of the new experiences. We can make this searching that the child does easier or harder depending on how we design our activities at school.

Usually we break up the curriculum into subjects, and the subjects into sections, and the goals for the day into particular items to be learned. This is spelling, this is writing, now we have reading, and maths, and drama, and physical education, social studies and nature study or science. Inside the child's head the connections are rather closely linked but we are always taking our subjects apart and teaching them in small pieces. Do our curricula and our timetables and our rules to be learned and our teaching sequences actually prevent connections being made by the child? I am sure they do. And the younger the child the less he can tolerate this fragmentation and the more trouble he has with putting the learning together.

To guard against such fragmentation we have to have *some* activities which focus many kinds of learning around one important topic. The child reads, talks, writes, paints, and makes things relating to a book shared, a theme for the week, an expedition that the class took, or a wall display constructed co-operatively. Activities like these put learning which we usually take apart together again.

That needs to happen in second language learning, and we need to plan to make it happen. What we have to learn to think about is how can we get multiple payoffs in learning from one activity in our programme.

How can we get children to actively work on learning what we want them to learn? How do we get the child to use his prior knowledge in the service of new knowledge? How do we get children to see connections between aspects of his school subjects? We have to have some activities which allow the child, learning in his mother tongue or another language, to use the knowledge of the world which he already has in his head in that activity. He needs to write about, and hear about the things he knows, when he is faced with a second language. He needs to read books about and talk about the things he already knows in that second language. In that way *meaningfulness* is retained. The meanings that he already understands are reworked in a new medium—another language.

Writing Down Messages

The New Zealand literacy programme for all children including the second language Pacific Island children in our schools like Tomai, has four facets. Firstly children are expected to write when they come to school and before they have been taught their letters or can read. They dictate little texts, sentences or stories about their personal experiences to the teacher who writes these down and the children 'read' them back. Soon they are writing some of the letters, or even words for themselves, and the teacher is helping only when necessary. Before very long they are doing some of the writing for themselves. Classrooms are a riot of writing and children who can re-read what they have written begin to read what others have written.

The messages are the children's messages, coming from their experiences. They may be very short, but they are written with care, re-read with pride and shared with others. From time to time the teacher adds a sample of the child's creative writing to the child's folder of work and that provides her assessment of progress. You can capture the changes in skill in these samples of work in the first year. In them you will discover that there is much to learn about scripts and writing text long before children know any words.

Reading to Children—Experience with Book Language

A second activity is reading to children as a first step towards them reading to themselves. About 1978 a little book called *"On The Way To Reading"* was distributed widely to parents of preschool children in my country. It contained advice like this.

Reading to children can give as much pleasure to parents as it does to children.

From the very time your child is big enough to climb on your knee, he will love to share books and nursery rhymes with you ... One of the best ways to get children interested in reading is to read to them yourself from enjoyable books.
Let them handle the books ...

Look at the pictures in books with your child.
Talk about them together. Ask him questions such as: "What's in the picture?", "Where do you think it's going?", "Why do you think it's doing that?", "What do you think it will do next?"

Children will choose their favourite stories to be read to them over and over again.

When you are reading to your child you may try to cheat now and then by turning over a couple of pages at once. It doesn't take long before you realise you can't do that anymore. Instead of you reading to your child, he is joining in with you, and becoming more and more familiar with the story ...

You will soon find he returns to his old favourites and "reads" them to himself. He will look at the pictures, turn the pages and repeat the story.

At first, this "reading" is often simply remembering the ideas in the story. The child puts these ideas together in his own words. This is a very important stage in learning to read.

By re-telling his favourite stories in his own way, a child learns many things. He finds out how to turn pages and grows used to the language in books. He develops his memory and learns to concentrate. He uses and understands more and more words and practices the things he has seen you do when you have read to him.

Some young children may learn to recognise a few words. However, this is not usual before they start school and it should not be expected of them. (Horton 1978)

There is much to be learned about the format and the conventions of stories even before the child learns any words.

The text goes on to explain to parents that teachers will share books with children, too.

Many teachers share books in a similar way in the classroom. The teacher reads with a group of children, rather than with one child. She holds the book so that all children can see the pictures and words. To make sure of this, some teachers make large copies of books that are favourites, or that they know will become favourites. These often have rhymes, or repeat words in patterns, as in:

I do not like green eggs and ham,
I do not like them, Sam-I-am.

Or

I meant what I said,
And I said what I meant.

An elephant's faithful,
One hundred percent.

> As the teacher reads aloud the children gradually join in, until they are reading with her. She will ask questions and encourage discussion about the book as they go along. She'll encourage them to guess what the book's about, what's going to happen next, and what may happen at the end. She'll pause now and then to encourage children to predict a word and help them check their guesses by getting them to tell her how they know. In this way children learn and practise many skills. (Horton 1978)

Shared book experience in classrooms was an approach developed by Holdaway (1979) in the multiethnic inner city schools of Auckland. The story-sharing model was at first based on the bed-time story model. The teaching conditions that he advocated were these:

> Read to the children in school in a way so that the print can be seen. Use enlarged print for listening and looking at stories and participating in all aspects of reading. Select some books that are favourites or will become favourites. Select simple stories without undue concern for vocabulary, have plenty of books like 20 for the first two weeks. Enlarged books are not all illustrated, nor polished pieces of work. The children will return to the trade book for their independent reading ... an emerging reader needs a battery of books that he can zoom through with joyous familiarity. Children not familiar with the syntactic patterns, idioms and tunes of English require the joyful repetition of a rich literature through the ear and across the tongue even more than children who have enjoyed this experience in their own homes and in their own vernacular ... so that the patterns of a book dialect are running through the automatic language system of the child. (Holdaway 1979, p. 194)

In New Zealand schools story books chosen according to their difficulty, for their memorable quality, high interest and special satisfactions in language, are 'enlarged' or 'blown up' into a 'big' version with big print that allows every child in a reading group to see the detail of letters and words. Enlarged text makes it possible for a large group of 6–8 children to participate and share in the pleasures of the story being read to them and at the same time enjoy a clear view of print detail.

The children sit in an informal group on the carpet in front of the easel with the teacher seated on a small chair to one side of the enlarged book. In this way all obtain a clear view.

The materials used for Shared Book Experiences are continuously and readily available for long periods in classroom so the children are able to return frequently to reread a wide variety of familiar material in this enlarged form.

In a recent UNESCO document an official description of the New Zealand programme stated that it is important for the child learning to read to hear books read. Books are not written in the same dialect that we use when we talk to one another. In the sharing children hear book language.

> The regular and frequent reading to the children of attractive story books of high literary quality ... is therefore an important feature of classroom programmes. (Leckie 1983)

Sharing books with children is an integral part of the school's programme. It is central and focal to increasing power over language and language variations. It is not entertainment—Reading to children leads (1) to discussion, (2) to re-reading, and (3) to independent reading of that book.

Let me briefly explore three development research projects which could be used to defend this position.

1. At the preschool level sharing books was used in a research study in a Maori preschool in Hamilton. Ritchie (1978) compared the progress of three groups of children on the Peabody Language program and the Distar program with a Book Experience program.

The teacher used questioning techniques to ensure that children were actively participating in story reading so that the story became a language extension experience.

The first books were chosen as particularly suitable for developing positive and negative statements. For example, from The Lion in the Meadow

> What is the boy doing?
>
> Can a boy dance? Cry? Sing? Fly?
>
> Is this boy singing? Running?

Books were chosen because they are good for predicting what will happen next.

> Over in the Meadow   Just in Time for the King's Birthday
> Goodnight Owl   My Cat Likes to Hide in Boxes

Books were chosen because they were suitable for 'why' questioning, for then you must also have a reason for your prediction, which is a step ahead.

> Whose Mouse Are You?   The Cat Who Thought He Was A Tiger
> Is This You?   Just Suppose

and so on.

Several days were spent in detailed discussion of the text and illustrations of the story so that the children came to have an inside knowledge of the book (and books in general), and a kind of power over it, which came from a familiarity that seemed to say, 'Now I know all about you. You are my servant, not my master.' The story was reread, acted and discussed and listened to through the listening post. Multiple copies were available. Stories were repeated so they could be kept in the memories of the group.

Children were being trained to link books with talking, making jokes, acting roles and all the fun of using words effectively and well. Book language is different from oral language and children who have contact with the language of books will find transitions in school easier than those whose language background is exclusively oral. I am not surprised that the assessed gains of the book sharing program were as great as those from a structured language kit.

> The children in the shared book experience programme made just as much progress as those who were taught by means of the American language development kits. (Ritchie 1978)

2. If you look at the *Reading Research Quarterly* for the last year you will find an account of how these ideas have been used in a careful piece of research completed by Elley and Mangubhai (1983) which tells how a reading programme based on shared book experience was used with village children in Fiji

who were nine and ten years. It increased the *oral* language scores of those children.
3. Research reports are available of a similar programme run on Niue Island in the South Pacific and studied by Elley before his Fiji study (1980).

What Should Be Happening

These are language activities. English is being heard in association with pictures. The meanings of language are being clarified by the teacher's questions and the children's discussions as meanings have pride of place in this activity. Prediction and anticipation are being encouraged as the story is brought to a stage of familiarity. In the child's retelling of the story the language of the book is being mingled with the language of the child, influencing it to change. So both *oral language* and *reading* are being taken care of in this situation.

A child who has limited control of English participates *earlier* in such language situations when his (likely to be) partly wrong responses are drowned in the group responses. In New Zealand there are no magical qualities attributed to "Big Books". They will not teach children to read. Big books display book conventions to groups of children, clearly. They provide a transitional tool to enhance the visual input from print during sharing time. They provide opportunities for re-reading in twos or threes or at the listening post. Those activities are also transitional because the end goal is to have the child read the book alone, and to be free to do this again and again. Re-reading enriches the initial experience.

Sharing books with children before *they* try to read them makes the task easier. They have some idea in their heads of the language that is to be used, they have a sense of the ideas and the plot and how the story should go (just as Tomai did).

Some of the strangeness of the book is made familiar. When this approach is taken for second language children they are able to approach more reading in a holistic way—they read text for its meanings. Otherwise, they could fall into the trap of believing that reading is only a matter of attending to letters and to words. Warwick Elley's work in the South Pacific islands of Fiji and Nuie supports this approach with second language children. *I am not speaking here of a whole programme but rather of a second important facet of a comprehensive programme.*

Reading Instruction

A third facet of the programme is the formal reading lessons, whatever programme you traditionally run. There may have to be some curtailing of these lessons to make room for other activities. It is important to take into account that the child will be doing important learning about reading in his writing activities and in shared book experience, in oral language and in dramatic play.

Teacher-Child Talk—A Fourth Component

A learner may make the most surprising links and not the ones the teacher had expected. This is to be valued; it is a sign of an active mind. The student has to learn actively to look for connections, to test what he finds against other connections, to weigh up the result and to accept or reject the solution, searching again if need be.

Dialogue between teacher and child is one way of helping children to search for connections. Not didactic teaching (which tries to put the child on the right path by correcting him) but conversation, exploring how the child understands a text.

Dialogue is where the understandings of the child and the teacher meet and connect. Then cultural mismatches are revealed. There are wide gulfs between what adults understand and what the child can make sense of. The gulfs are narrowed when the adult tries to see what connections the child is making.

Joan Tough comments on this.

> The skills that are developed through the experiences of participating in dialogue are those skills of thinking and using language that would seem to provide the very basis from which education should proceed. (Tough 1977, p. 76)

There is a sound rationale here for sharing books and talking about the child's view of those books or for allowing time for a conference about a book the child has read in which the lead is taken by the child reader. For these reasons it is important to create contexts in school in which dialogue can take place. The formal environment of school should be modified to promote a need to communicate and to give time to conversation.

Acting and Story-Telling—Further Bridges to Language Gains

What occurred in Warwick Elley's research in Fiji is analogous to what occurred in the following case study. There is an account of learning by American kindergarten children written by Vivian Paley, called *Wally's Stories*. It is a delight. Her barely articulate children learn to tell stories and have their classmates act those stories. The teacher helps the children discover more and more about themselves and their worlds including inventing pulleys and measuring the relative size of two carpets by lying children down on them to discover that one took five children and the other only four. That dialogue is hilarious.

My quote, however, is of a girl with little English who came through story-telling to risk expressing her ideas in English before others. Listen to this case report of language change through acting and story-telling.

"Akemi does not permit herself mistakes," her father had said on the first day of school, "so she won't practice English." He watched his daughter as she sat alone, drawing with her new school crayons. "If she learned English better she wouldn't be so disagreeable with the children. She was so angry when the nursery school children did not understand her."

The Nakamotos had come to America from Japan the year before. They were disappointed with Akemi's adjustment to school. "In Japan she loved school," Mr. Nakamoto continued. "She reads and writes in Japanese like a seven-year-old."

Mr. Nakamoto was right about Akemi. She was not comfortable with the children and she was afraid to speak English. What neither of us foresaw was the speed with which she began to use English in order to act in a play.

The first character she wanted to be was the woman in *The Funny Little Woman*. This Japanese folktale concerns an old woman's attempt to retrieve a rice dumpling that rolls through a crack in the earth down to a place where "statues of the gods" live alongside monstrous creatures called "wicked oni." The old woman tricks the oni, steals their magic rice paddle, and returns safely to the world above.

The old woman's habit of saying "tee-hee-hee" made Akemi laugh despite a determined effort to remain the solemn outsider. She took the role immediately and produced a barely audible "tee-hee-hee", but it was enough to make her wish for more.

"Read me," she would insist, following me around with the book in her hands. Each time I read the story, Akemi repeated more of the dialogue. "My dumpling, my dumpling! Has anyone seen my dumpling?" became Akemi's leitmotif. She had accomplished her first complete English sentence, and since everyone knew the story she did not have to explain herself further.

By Monday of the second week, Akemi was ready to add to her repertoire. She walked directly to the library corner and began leafing through a pile of books. When she came to A Blue Seed, our only other Japanese story, she examined it carefully.

"If I be this? She asked, pointing to the fox.

"Can I be the fox?" I repeated her question.

"If I can be fox?" she asked again.

"Yes, you can. We'll read the book at piano time.".…

I took four Japanese stories out of the library, but Akemi, after a quick glance, passed them by. Her commitment was not to Japanese stories but to magic. She wanted characters who looked the way she wanted to look and said what she needed to say.

In Tico and the Golden Wings, the wishingbird said the right words for Akemi. "I am the wishingbird. Make a wish and it will come true.".…

"Drakestail" gave Akemi a couplet she liked even better. "Quack, quack, quack, when shall I get my money back?" Akemi carried her memorized lines around like gifts, bestowing them on children in generous doses. "Quack, quack, quack, when shall I get my money back?" she would say, dipping a brush into a jar of paint. Soon everyone at the painting table would be chanting along with her.

"I am the wishingbird," she said, flying gracefully into the doll corner. "I wish for a golden crown," Jill responded, whereupon Akemi delicately touched her head with an invisible wand.

Adults who go about quoting poetry seldom receive encouragement, but the children rewarded Akemi by repeating her phrases and motions. She correctly interpreted this as friendship. Whenever a child copied her, Akemi would say, "Okay. You friend of me."

Her triumph came just before Halloween. She wanted a witch story but none of the Halloween stories pleased her. She told the librarian, "Witch story but not Halloween," and was given Strega Nona, an Italian folktale about a kindly old witch who owns a magic pasta pot.

Akemi memorized the magic verse at home.

Bubble bubble, pasta pot,

Boil me up some pasta, nice and hot.

I'm hungry and it's time to sup,

Boil enough pasta to fill me up.

Wally came running over. "What's that from, Akemi?"

"Witch book not Halloween," she replied. "You can read."

"I can't read yet," said Wally. "Mrs. Paley'll read it to us."

By the end of the day almost everyone knew the entire verse, and Akemi was ready to tell her first story. "Now I telling story, okay?" In only six weeks, Akemi had become a story-teller in English. "Is Halloween story," she began.

One day four colors walking. But one witch sees four colors. Witch with four hands. Witch holds four colors. "Let go, let go!" Four colors running. Witch running. Four colors running home. Is mother. Oh, good.

In Akemi's next story just two weeks later, she had made considerable progress.

One day is magic cherry tree. A nice skeleton is coming. The cherry tree says, "We are playing," A black cloud is coming. The cherry tree says, "They are playing all day." The mother comes. "You are coming home."

On Rose's birthday, in January Akemi dictated a story to be acted out at Rose's party. "Rose is the magic princess," she told us.

Once there is castle has everything. Even nine princesses and nine dogs ... But then the bad king came and stole the magic princess but she is not afraid. The king is magic but she makes him unmagic so he can't use his magic. She makes him into a frog and makes herself into a magic shark and she ate up his castle. Then the good-guy prince comes back and she makes him magic too so he is never afraid forever.

Akemi was conquering English, and I was learning an important principle: magic can erase the experiential differences between children ... When magic is accepted and encouraged, the children are not afraid to think and speak. (Paley 1981, pp. 122–126)

Compare the wholeness of Akemi's experiences with this language learning lesson from a British classroom of six year olds—a good lesson, *of its kind!*, carefully recorded by Mills (1980, p. 57).

T: Right. Here's a pencil. The pencil is in the tin. The brush is in the cup (Actions and objects are used.) The scissors, the scissors are in the box. The crayon is in the box. The crayon is in the box. Now, Balvant, tell me about the pencils.

Ch: Pencils in the tin.
T: They're in the tin. Right.
Ch: They're in the tin.
T: Inderjit, tell me about the brush.
Ch: In the cup.
T: It's in the cup. It's in the cup.
Ch: It's in the cup.
T: Tell me about the crayon. Tell me about the crayon.
Ch: The crayon's on.
Ch: The crayon's in the cup.
T: The crayon's in the box. It's in the box.
Ch: Box.
Ch: It's in the box.
T: It's in the box. It's in the box.
Ch: It's in the box.
T: You say it. Good. It's in the box.
Ch: It's in the box.
T: Good. Tell me about the scissors.
Ch: It's in the box.
T: (Whispers) They, they. They're in the box.
Ch: They're in the box.
T: Right. They're in the box. In. Now all those things are in. In. In. Now then. Where's my hand?
Ch: On the table.
Ch: On the table.
T: Right. My hand's on the table. The picture's on the wall. That picture's on the wall. This picture's …
Ch: On the wall.
T: … On the board. On the board.
Ch: On the blackboard
T: My coat, it's …
Ch: On, on …
T: … on the peg
Ch: On the peg
T: The bin, it's …
Ch: On the floor
T: … On the floor. It's on the floor Right.

   I would recommend that much (but not all) of such structured linguistic teaching of language be transferred for the young child to the writing, shared book and discussion sessions of primary grade activities and lessons such as these be used (rarely), to address any persisting problems noted by the teacher.
   This brings me back to the texts available for children to read.

Natural Language Texts, Contrived Texts and Literary Texts

A teacher who shares books with children will need to know how difficult her books are. She will need to work out a gradient of difficulty among the stories she shares with her pupils. Some have easier language than others and should be introduced first. Trade books can have a literary kind of language that is too hard for new-comers to the language.

On the other hand books written as reading texts with a controlled vocabulary may *look* simple but they do not teach the children English that is the kind of English we use when we speak. They use a contrived form of English. We would not want our child to talk the way basal readers are written.

A third kind of text is helpful here. It is a natural language text. It is written in the kind of language that children of five to seven years use in their mother tongue. It is children's language or close to it.

Natural language texts allow the very young child to predict what will occur in books without the demands of bookish kinds of language (as in literary texts) or contrived kinds of language (as in basal readers). Language that rises naturally to the child's tongue is what the author uses. It is written the way that children speak.

Sam's Mask is an easy early natural language reading text, unpretentious but the language sounds to me like child language. The pictures are delightful.

Sam made a mask.

He made eyes.

He made a big mouth.

He made a nose.

He made long hair.

Sam took the mask home after school.

He knocked on the door.

"Help!" said Mum.

"Who's this monster wearing Sam's pants?". (Cachemaille 1983)

Number One is a ghost story, illustrated very effectively black and white. The text is very much like everyday speech.

It is night.

The ghost comes

out of his cupboard,

out of his house

and into the town.

"Who can I boo?" he says.

Look!

Here comes a man in a taxi.

"He'll do," says the ghost.

The taxi stops,

and the man jumps out.

"Boo!" says the ghost.

"Oooo! A horrible, horrible ghost!"

says the man,

and he runs away.

"Number One!" says the ghost.

(Cowley 1982).

Before long the child is gaining experience with book dialect and a gradual transition is made from natural language texts supported only by the language the child previously controlled to texts which contain a little more of the literary flourishes that teach him something new about book language. I have tried to select a text which I think is making that kind of transition. It is called *The Great Grumbler and the Wonder Tree*.

Mrs. Finch was a good gardener

and Mr. Finch was a great grumbler.

Whenever Mrs. Finch grew something

and cooked it for his tea,

Mr. Finch always said

he would rather have something else.

When she cooked carrots,

he said he would rather have cabbage.

When she cooked cabbage,

he sighed and asked for corn.

He said "Yuck!" to her parsnips

and "Poof!" to her pumpkins.

(Then someone gave Mrs. Finch a wonder seed.)

Mrs. Finch planted the wonder tree seed

by her back door.

She fed it well.

She watered it well.

And she weeded it very well.

(By the time we get to the last page a more literary style has taken over.)

While Mr. Finch was doing the dishes,

Mrs. Finch went out to the wonder tree,

and watered it carefully.

She gave it lovely leaf mould

and weeded around its toes.

"You're a good friend to me," she said.

"I can see he won't do much more grumbling

with you to help me."

And neither he did!

(Mahy 1984).

The last line presents a challenge to the young reader—a small challenge but a challenge nonetheless.

And So, To Conclude

Whichever language we are teaching the child to read, to write or to speak we need to use the child's prior knowledge in the service of the new learning. The child's world is full of meaningful experiences and our activities can be related to these to enlist child-power to get learning gains. If the language is new to the child there is so much to learn that it would be foolish to divorce the activities from the only thing the child can bring to these activities—meaning, drawn from his understanding of the world and how things work.

Whether he is learning literacy in his first or second language the child needs to write about things he knows and wants to write about, to have stories read to him which he can understand at his level of oral language and which will extend that control, to be encouraged to re-tell, or act, or discuss, or re-read those stories, and be given planned opportunities to hear the language aloud, and to go back over it independently in the last phase of mastery.

For some of these activities you will want to write natural language texts, or find them, or construct them with children's help. Remember this important and reassuring fact—there is a vocabulary control in natural language. Every language has some words that occur more frequently than others. Frequency is an inbuilt vocabulary control in the language and leads to a gradual and increasing control over frequently occurring words. The child from two cultures will need to be given learning opportunities which allow him to bring these two cultures together in some way. Tomai provides an example of this.

Tomai tried to retell *Goldilocks and the Three Bears* in the words of the text. "Too hard" he said, "Can I tell you Goldilocks out of my head?" Wisely the interviewer agreed and he told a good tale. It is the ending that I want you to hear because of its delightful cultural connections as Goldilock's parents take action to straighten out the social etiquette of the situation. Tomai has the opportunity to make the necessary social adjustments.

...and Goldilocks ran home to mummy. And she said,

"Mummy, I was naughty." "Oh, you shouldn't go there,

little Goldilocks, I will give you a hard smack.

Smack, smack." And father came home from work and

he boot the little Goldilocks harder and harder...

And then he said, "We're going to go there *tomorrow*."

And they went there and Mother got some porridge and

some apples and the little Goldilocks got some bananas.

And so, knock, knock, "Who's that?" "It's only the

big man." "Come in right now." And he hammered away.

And the little Goldilocks said to her daddy, "Can I

play with little baby bear?" "Of course you can."

And they went out saying, "Bye-bye."

What an interesting way for a little five year old Cook Island Polynesian boy to end a story in his second language and culture, giving it the kind of resolution that his first culture would require—taking food to the neighbours to restore good relations and mending the broken chair. *He* could solve the problem of cultural differences. Educationally, it seems to me to be very important that somebody gave him the opportunity to do that.

Acknowledgements With kind permission from Taylor and Francis Ltd (http://www.tandfonline. com) and National Institute of Education (Singapore): Beginning Literacy in Two Languages, Marie M. Clay, Singapore Journal of Education, Volume 7, Issue 2, page 3–14, published online 13 March 2008, http://www.tandfonline.com/10.1080/02188798508547601, copyright © National Institute of Education, Singapore, reprinted by permission of Taylor & Francis Ltd, http://www. tandfonline.com on behalf of National Institute of Education, Singapore.

References

Cachemaille, C. (1983). *Sam's mask. Ready to Read*. Wellington, New Zealand: Department of Education.
Cowley, J. (1982). *Number One. Ready to Read*. Wellington, New Zealand: Department of Education.

Elley, W. B. (1980). A comparison of content-interest and structuralist reading programmes in Niue primary schools. *New Zealand Journal of Educational Studies, 15*(1), 39–53.

Elley, W. B., & Mangubhai, F. (1983). The impact of reading on second language learning. *Reading Research Quarterly, 19*(1), 53–67.

Holdaway, D. (1979). *The foundations of literacy*. Sydney, Australia: Ashton Scholastic.

Horton, J. (1978). *On the way to reading*. Wellington, New Zealand: School Publications Branch, Department of Education in conjunction with the Continuing Education Unit, Radio New Zealand.

Kagan, J. (1971). *Understanding children: Behaviour, motives and thought*. New York, NY: Harcourt Brace Jovanovich.

Leckie, N. (1983). *Textbooks and reading materials. Volume One: The Ready to Read project: The New Zealand experience*. Bangkok, Thailand: UNESCO Regional Office for Education in Asia and the Pacific.

Mahy, M. (1984). *The great grumbler and the wonder tree. Ready to Read*. Wellington, New Zealand: Department of Education.

Mills, R. W. (1980). *Classroom observation of primary school children*. London, England: George Allen & Unwin.

Paley, V. G. (1981). *Wally's stories*. Cambridge, MA: Harvard University Press.

Ritchie, J. (1978). *Chance to be equal*. Queen Charlotte Sound, New Zealand: Cape Catley.

Rodriguez, R. (1982). *Hunger of memory: The education of Richard Rodriguez: An autobiography*. Boston, MA: D.R. Godine.

Stirling, E. (1980). *Eruera: The teachings of a Maori Elder as told to Anne Salmond*. Wellington, New Zealand: Oxford University Press.

Tough, J. (1977). *The development of meaning*. London, England: George Allen & Unwin.

Author Biography

Dr. Marie Mildred Clay majored in education at the University of New Zealand earning a bachelor's degree in 1946 and a master's degree in 1948. She studied child psychology at the University of Minnesota and received her Ph.D. from the University of Auckland in 1966. She was on the Faculty since 1960. She was a distinguished researcher known for her work in global educational literacy and was very committed to the idea that children who struggle to learn to read and write can be helped with early intervention. She developed the Reading Recovery intervention programme which was adopted by all New Zealand schools in 1983. The programme was used in Great Britain, Canada, Australia, New Zealand and the United States. In 1982 she was inducted into the International Reading Association's Reading Hall of Fame. She served as a Distinguished Visiting Scholar at the Faculty at Ohio State University 1984–1985. In recognition of Marie Clay's service and successful leadership in literacy education, in 1987 she was made a Dame Commander of the Order of the British Empire by Queen Elizabeth II. In 1992 she was elected president of the International Reading Association. She passed away on 13 April 2007 at the age of 81.

Chapter 2
A Vision of Education in the 21st Century

Ungku Abdul Aziz

I am greatly honoured with this invitation to deliver the Ruth Wong Memorial Lecture.

I have warm memories of the late Professor Ruth Wong who was an able member of the Faculty of Education at the University of Malaya from its inception. She was not only a friendly and constructive person but she had a far-sighted vision that will be, I hope, somewhat evoked during the course of my lecture this evening.

We should begin, like travellers in the jungle. We have to clear the way. While we may share a common terminology, we may not have the same connotation for certain concepts, especially when they are placed in the context of the future.

In the first place I have limited my discussion to what I consider to be a possible situation in the next century in a developing country like Singapore or Malaysia.

With some adjustments, mainly for time differences and warp-lag (not jet lag) it could equally be a vision for the other countries in the ASEAN region, provided they are stacked in some order of progress, especially in the field of education.

I am offering you a vision quite dispassionately—like any science fiction writer. I am presenting you with a possible view. It is not necessarily the future that I would recommend. It may be or it may not be. As they say in lateral thinking, we shall seek movement not judgement.

I am describing a possible future especially in the field of education that is likely to occur some time in the 21st century. Most of the elements necessary for the realisation of that future are already available in the laboratories or are actually being practised in some countries like Japan or parts of Europe. The only really fantastic part is the Time-bound Mass Rapid Transit Vehicle (TBMRTV). The rest is already around somewhere or waiting to be adopted more extensively.

I would like to clarify and emphasise one point. In everything that I shall discuss this evening the overriding principle will be that all issues and problems should be

U.A. Aziz (✉)
University of Malaya, Kuala Lumpur, Malaysia
e-mail: farrah@azair.com.my

© Springer Nature Singapore Pte Ltd. 2017
O.S. Tan et al. (eds.), *Global Voices in Education*,
DOI 10.1007/978-981-10-3539-5_2

seen in a state of complexity—taking the term complexity in its technical, philo-sophical sense. Simply this means that every issue will be subject to a considerable variety of influences that are occurring at different rates of change and are exerting different rates of pressure.

We shall begin our list of introductory concepts with a consideration of time and the pace of change.

At an international meeting I attended last year in Paris, we were addressing major problems that the world was likely to face in the year 2000. As meetings consisting largely of academics go—someone asked, "Why take the year 2000 and not 2001 or 1999?" With tongue in cheek I pointed out that the figure 2000 was based on the Christian-European calendar that itself had been adjusted several times. One could have taken the Chinese calendar with its infinite number of 60-year cycles or the Thai calendar or the Islamic calendar. Happily we agreed by consensus that the year 2000 AD would be a convenient milestone for addressing the fate of mankind.

Nevertheless, here I feel we do not need a benchmark for a period that will begin just over a decade away.

Therefore tonight let me invite you to accompany me on a journey into the future that will take us to some period of time within the 21st century.

And since this is Singapore, I have not brought down my magic carpet. I shall ask you to ride the specially created magic coaches of the TBMRTV to go on a journey into the 21st century. Please remember it is the journey that is important, not the technical descriptions of the stations that we may pass by during our journey into the 21st century.

For reasons of economy of time we shall travel mainly on the education line. For purposes of constructing a multi-dimensional image we shall try to view education in relation to three other lines: health, cultural and social development, and eco-nomic growth.

For convenience we shall assume the rates of economic and social progress are fairly steady, that there is exceptional political stability and that current trends in population growth will continue.

I apologise for using this economist's approach to simplify what I have already described as a complex situation. However, as in the case of the MRT you can only ride in one direction at one time.

We are in a position to begin our journey. We shall first look at some broad features of the educational system in the future.

There will be at least four striking differences from the present:

(1) Education will be mind training rather than knowledge accumulation and skill learning.
(2) Life long education will dissolve the current divisions of the education system which are structured to provide cut-off points or shunting facilities at different age levels of students: kindergarten, primary and secondary school, college and university, etc. Education may begin in the womb and continue until death of the brain.

(3) Life will be leisurely, according to our current understanding of the term lei-
    sure. Work will be a pleasure. That is, at least work involving physical effort or
    manipulative dexterity.
(4) In health the common aim will be the care of the human body and the mind in
    such a way that sickness is utterly minimised. Doctors of today who live by
    diagnosis, prescription, treatment and surgery will evolve into health carers
    who strive to eliminate diseases and direct people on the way to a long and
    active healthy life.

With this foundation we can now slow down our TBMRTV so that we can catch
a vision of education at some time in the 21st century.

You may recall that I have suggested that education is likely to be lifelong. I will
add that it will be universal. Some of you may now be raising your hackles. For
example, you may be asking, "where can so many institutions of higher learning be
located?".

To understand this we have to assume that at least two criteria will be met.

(a) People do not have to leave the world of learning to seek employment; and
(b) Technology will provide access to learning in most convenient ways.

These are key topics so let me elaborate them before we go any further.
We can have lifelong learning if we can provide three things:

 (i) appropriate technology for access and delivery;
 (ii) global links to the banks of knowledge and timeliness in the dissemination of
      new knowledge;
(iii) an education system that aims to develop minds and not to fill memories with
      data that are frequently obsolete or to provide training in certain types of
      dexterity which may not be needed by many people.

In this vision of the 21st century, please do not misunderstand me—learning
may be open to any subject. Learners, i.e. all the people, will seek to develop their
minds so that they can enjoy a full life of the mind and help bring progress to those
who are still behind them in development while they push forward their own
frontiers of knowledge.

The good news is that exams of any kind will no longer be necessary. There will
be no particular jobs with specific requirements so paper qualifications will be
useless.

Everybody can learn whatever he or she wishes to learn from the culture of the
Aztecs to the philosophies of the Mongols, from the art of Leonardo da Vinci to
molecular psychology.

How will this become possible? Technology already links research centres of
institutions of higher learning in this part of the world with similar institutions in the
most advanced countries. Fibre optics and satellites will enable any enquiring mind
to gain access not only to any bank of knowledge anywhere including the latest
information, but people will be able to communicate with (the fashionable term is
interface with) any scholar anywhere on the globe.

Dedicated computers will provide voice activated translation facilities that will allow a Singaporean speaking English or Chinese to discuss a topic in Mongolian with someone located in Ulan Bator.

All the books and journals, i.e. all the information available in all forms of printed materials, tapes and other types of storage in great centres such as the Library of Congress or the British Library, not to mention specialised collections in our own libraries will be available to everybody on a global basis.

The learners at home will be able to produce hard copies through a kind of super fax machine that reproduces in colour or on a large screen located on a wall. We already see this in interactive self-learning using laser disks and personal computers.

If a learner needs to compare the murals of the Ajanta caves in India with the carvings in Borbordor in Java, she can call up both on a split screen in three dimensions and select commentaries from a bibliography that will appear on her visual display unit (VDU).

If on a rainy evening, someone wishes to listen to *Divertimento in E-flat major, K.563* by Mozart, he can call up a presentation by a trio who will be playing with instruments that are close copies of the original instruments. A bonus from this is that people who like music or dance will no longer be so narrow minded as to believe that Western chamber music is high classical style while the Johore *ghazal* is merely folk music.

When you acquire a dwelling at that time, all the necessary equipment will be built-in, in the same way as kitchens and bathrooms are built-in today.

Today, we believe that competition is the best way to allow the fittest talents to float up to the top. This is also known as meritocracy. We are inclined to believe that all citizens do have equal opportunities to participate in the overall system. While this may be true for some countries, extreme differences of location can create handicaps that reduce the equality of access or of opportunity. In the future men will be wiser and technology will provide genuine opportunities to all so that facilities are really equitably distributed. The social and education system will create a political system that should be harmonious with the widespread dispersion of opportunities for learning.

As there are hierarchies of nations today, so there will continue to be hierarchies of nations in the future. On the time scale of progress there will be advanced nations, less advanced nations and least advanced nations. A big difference between now and then is that the opportunities for closing the gaps between the levels of progress will be greater and more effective because of technological progress and new systems of education.

The attitudes of the advanced nations will no longer be based on national self-interest above all with the ends justifying the means. Like some popular artists of today, peoples of the world will learn to see the global population as one family of man. The more fortunate members will help the less fortunate members to enjoy a life of the mind rather than to suffer a life of trying to fill the stomach.

What will be the role of teachers or professors in such a world? The guru will be accorded the place he had 400–1000 years ago in this part of the world. He will be among the wisest of the wise, not someone who has to publish or perish regardless of quality, neither does he have to kowtow to the powers that be. In his turn, he will be utterly devoted to the pursuit of knowledge in every excellent way possible. The guru will be rewarded with respect and love to an extent hitherto unknown.

Compared to the present, his status could be compared to a cross between a pop-star and the president of a large multi-national corporation. That is the guru of the future. Among the aspirants to the position of guru will be mind workers who will be studying the past and imagining the future for the benefit of mankind.

At this point I will reduce the speed of our magic vehicle and remind you that we are participating in a vision of a different world. This could be the reality for our future generations in the same way as the world of this Island has become and was totally unimaginable by the residents of this place 200 years ago.

I decided to avoid peppering this talk with quotations but I will make one exception to remind you of one man of the 1960s who tried hard to create the intellectual apparatus for viewing the rest of this century. He is Marshall McLuhan, a guru of his time now bypassed by new academic fashions. In his book, "The Medium is the Massage: An Inventory of Effects" published in 1967 he said:

> All media work us over completely. They are so pervasive in their personal, political, economic, aesthetic, psychological, moral, ethical, and social consequences that they leave no part of us untouched, unaffected, unaltered. The medium is the massage. Any understanding of social and cultural change is impossible without a knowledge of the way media work as environments. (McLuhan and Fiore 1967, p. 26)

All media are extensions of some human faculty—psychic or physical. The wheel is an extension of the foot. The book is an extension of the eye. Clothing is an extension of the skin. Electric circuitry is an extension of the central nervous system. Media, by altering the environment, evoke in us unique ratios of sense perceptions. The extension of any one sense alters the way we think and act, the way we perceive the world. When these ratios change, men change.

Our electrically-configured world has forced us to move from the habit of data classification to the mode of pattern recognition. Lateral thinking says patterns of thinking get the mind imprisoned in logic bubbles and our problem is to find techniques to escape into new patterns. We continue with the quotation:

> Print technology created the public. Electric technology created the mass. The public consists of separate individuals walking around with separate fixed points of view. The new technology demand that we abandon the luxury of this pastime, this fragmentary outlook. (McLuhan and Fiore 1967, pp. 68–69)

Remember this was written just around the mid-point of this century some 25 years ago.

Today we can look forward to an educational system that really opens windows of the minds so that people can pursue happiness without the need of exploiting others. People can become educated and live in such a society that the good life is the life of the good mind and the good mind is developed by total life education. Such an education will not be fragmented by artificial boundaries of science and arts, biology and microbiology. Once education is free from the need to fill the learners' memories with cow dungs, then total life education can induce into tender minds from the earliest stages a few weeks after conception right through a long life. Imagine 100 years of unfolding of the 10 billion neurons of the brain. These expanded minds could mould the education system to do an even better task of mind building and so on ad infinitum.

In the future it may be that education will not be the only facility that will have a rather novel approach. In this lecture I have selected health as the other area to balance education. I fully realise that there are many areas that deserve equal attention. They could include transportation, energy, crime, environments, relations with other countries and so on. However, I have to make some selection and I believe that health is one of the major areas that will have an interacting and cumulative relationship with education that is equally significant to any of the other areas and so I have decided to discuss it.

The philosophy of health systems in the 21st century may be different from that prevailing now. While this new approach may not seem so different to those concerned with the system of Chinese medicine, nevertheless we could expect a diametrical change in the approach to sickness and health.

I realise that what I am about to say is somewhat controversial and I apologise in advance if I seem to be stepping on anyone's toes. However, I do want to recall a point that has been frequently discussed in literature on the subject.

For the majority of those who are concerned with sickness and its treatment, attention is directed to the provision of excellent facilities for diagnosis and treatment of sickness. Treatment is mainly based on the provision of medicines or the performance of surgery. Many fine doctors receive considerable material rewards because they are able to offer these services to the public.

A certain amount of public funds are devoted towards the so-called preventive measures that protect the public from the scourges of epidemics, sexually transmitted diseases (STD) or acquired immune deficiency syndrome (AIDS) and from the purveyors of foodstuffs that are unhygienically prepared.

Let me try to insure my welcome here by saying that my examples are drawn from experience in other countries rather than from Singapore.

Very little attention is given to schemes to keep the population so healthy that it does not become sick. In fact, the private sector is already beginning to tap a certain market by introducing health farms, clubs and gymnasiums. In Singapore and in some cities in Malaysia, it is delightful to see members of the public jogging on roads and in parks but these are still minority groups. Life expectancy tables and statistical patterns of the causes of death indicate that major changes will have to occur before virtually the whole population can be turned into healthy beings who have a life expectancy of a century.

In education there will be health education of such quality that proper nutrition and exercise will be seen to be part of a normal life. People in the future will find it incredible that their forebears, half a century earlier, were ready to consume food and drugs that were rendering them prone to disease and damaging their bodies.

How will the changes in education that we have looked at in some detail and the changes in health systems that we have barely touched on, influence the social and cultural domain as well as the pattern of the economy in the future?

My guess is that instead of having one fruit salad of a culture we will have a population who have the capacity to enjoy a great variety of aesthetic experiences. Many will be able to participate directly in fine arts performances. They may, in fact return to the Renaissance man like Benvenut Cellini or Omar Khayam—men who were experts in several fields—music, mathematics, astronomy and poetry, etc. Quite unlike our present day so-called specialists who aspire to know more and more about less and less until they know everything about nothing.

They may adopt the philosophy of Lao Tsu—Be like water, fit in with everything, be soft yet strong.

Remember in the future society there will no longer be the need to have hidden persuaders or brain cleaning because everybody's mind will be well expanded.

I have taken the term culture in its widest connotation. With the assistance of some of the technologies that I have referred to and others that we can barely imagine today, it should be possible for any individual, in Singapore for example, to learn about and come to appreciate and even to participate at a distance on a karaoke type of arrangement in a great variety of cultural events from many parts of the world and from many civilizations that have existed at different times. Cultural appreciation in the future may be much more than a group of tourists being shown in versions of the natives performing so-called jazzed-up native dances in costumes that appear exotic so that they can be photographed by cameras draped around the tourists' necks. Tourism will begin in the living room and could be a total experience rather than descending and mounting buses to the monologues of tourist guides.

Progress in methods of reproduction will allow the schools and museums of the world to have faithful copies of the great works of art from all times. Youth will be as familiar with Byzantine icons as they are with the Persian poetry inscribed on Moghul paintings. It is possible that the sensibilities of the denizens of the 21st century may be so expanded that they will be able to experience and appreciate experiences so fine as to be inconceivable today.

Please remember this and kindly excuse me for not being able to describe the culture of the 21st century in detail because I have not yet had the opportunity to visit the place or the time. Indeed, it may be that if I went there I may not want to come back or the journey may only be available on a one-way ticket.

We could sum up the topic of culture in the 21st century by saying that people would have certain attitudes of mind as a result of the education system. Because of knowledge and training, people would have better control of their emotions. People would not have to spend so much of their time preparing for employment or working as we know it today. In our language they would have an abundance of leisure time. They would use this time for cultural activities. Gambling, drugs and crime would be things of the past. Education and the patterns of cultural life would render them obsolete and totally undesired by the citizens of the future.

Does this seem to you to be a rather boring future? It is all a question of perspectives. If you are looking at cultural life in the 21st century through the windows of our TBMRTV then it may appear to be rather unexciting. However, from the point of view of the people who are living around the tracks, the feeling may be quite different. They have a totally different perspective, and they may view our civilization in the 20th century as nasty, superficial and lacking in sincerity. This would not be too different from the way we see the world of the Dark Ages in Europe or in Asia. It is all a question of perspectives.

Finally, what can we say about the economy. As you might guess it will be a cashless economy. Not even plastic money will be needed. All the material goods needed can be produced by sophisticated robots or androids. All the drudgery will be taken care of by automatic machines that will be able not only to produce continuously but will be able to do their own maintenance and repair and reproduce themselves with improvements as time goes by. These are machines that can think. The next generation computers will eliminate the need for interest rates and wages differentials, there will not be any market place. This is not utopian, it is simply a world that is already beginning to happen in certain parts of the globe.

The issues of today that receive mainly lip service will be realised and mankind will come to understand that he lives in one global village and he has only one environment for the whole earth. The great economic problems of today will become interesting episodes in history. Perhaps people of the 21st century will be much puzzled as to how such a civilization could survive for as long as it did.

International indebtedness and exploitation of poor countries by the more affluent will disappear as will such trends as continuously worsening terms of trade wherein the industrialised economies take advantage of the primary producing countries. The technology that has facilitated the Big Bang and linked up a global stock exchange with occasional lapses into black days, crashes and shocks will evolve into a smooth system where all can enjoy the produce of the earth and no one has to live in fear or in poverty.

We have sampled a vision of the 21st century. We have not been able to know exactly where in the 21st century this vision may reflect reality. However, on one thing we can be certain: tomorrow will arrive by stealth. It will not arrive as one big bang and then we are there.

People of the future will have a different approach to all human interaction or negotiation. These people will no longer seek confrontation and contradiction as the means to find the truth and what is right, they will practice eclectics—that is constructive discussion, mushawarah (consensus) and the Japanese approach to discussions as it is done now. There will be no need for conflict big or small. There will be an abundance of discussion but it will be constructive and not destructive.

In conclusion, can we really journey into that beautiful part of the 21st century or will we be shunted into some dark hell that will be a prelude to the end of this earth as we know it? I am optimistic that wisdom will prevail and that our descendants will be wise and will truly enjoy the long life of the mind in a state of happiness and health.

Reference

McLuhan, M., & Fiore, Q. (1967). *The medium is the massage: An inventory of effects.* New York, NY: Bantam Books.

Author Biography

Royal Professor Ungku Abdul Aziz was elected Emeritus Professor of Economics by the University of Malaya in 1988. He is a well known economist in the Malaysian community. He completed his Bachelor of Arts degree (Honours) in Economics in the University of Malaya in Singapore and obtained his Doctor of Economics from Waseda University, Tokyo. In 1952, Ungku Aziz commenced his career in the University of Malaya as a Lecturer in Economics; obtained full professorship; became the Dean of the Faculty of Arts, and then Dean of the Faculty of Economics and Administration. In 1968, Professor Ungku Aziz ascended to the helm of the university as Vice Chancellor of the University of Malaya, becoming both the first Malaysian and the longest serving person to hold the post. He was a vigorous proponent of the use of the national language in education as a unifying factor, as well as a language of academia and research, while stressing that mastery in English was essential for academic excellence. He was conferred the title "Royal Professorship" in 1978. He retired as Vice Chancellor in 1988. Professor Ungku Aziz was responsible for much research in attempting to address domestic poverty. The subject, being dear to his heart, has spurred him to research the root causes of rural poverty in Malaysia, as well as identifying methods by which to alleviate poverty. He was also one of the founding members of the Malaysian Economic Association, a think tank dedicated to discussing Malaysian economic issues. In recognition of his career as an outstanding academician and his contributions to society, Professor Ungku Aziz has been bestowed with numerous awards and honours, including the Ordre des Arts et des Lettres (France), the Grand Cordon of the Order of the Sacred Treasure (Japan) and the Tun Abdul Razak Foundation Award (Malaysia). He has also received many honorary degrees from universities worldwide. After retirement in 1988 Ungku Aziz holds directorships in several companies and continues to be involved in many national and international institutions.

Chapter 3
Music Education for National Development: The Philippine Experience

Lucrecia R. Kasilag

I am most privileged to be invited to participate in this year's Dr. Ruth Wong's Memorial Lectures. As the first director of the Institute of Education, Dr. Wong made an invaluable contribution to the educational development of this country, which should provide a veritable source of inspiration to all of us committed educators.

Music embraces all aspects of human life in its potential and distinctive role of enriching and developing the totality of the human being. How he feels and thinks, what beliefs and plans he holds by which he makes proper decisions for his general well-being. To reach his goals and horizons the artist with characteristic vigour is emboldened to aspire for what is sublime and meaningful in his artistic and intellectual personality.

In the face of the present concentration on the scientific and technological advance in civilization, the educative processes have tended to put more stress on a competent professional and effective political being, rather than a sensitive and sensible individual aware of his surroundings and the need to uplift the human spirit above mere materialism. Thus, the measure of a true artist is what he does in his involvement with his own culture, resulting in his yearnings for the refinement of life and the search for the verity of identity.

In the concept of education in music and music in education, the humanist approach is essential in the development of a responsive studentry towards raising the consciousness to the truth and beauty of a country's heritage and traditional folk culture. By this approach, a generation of responsible citizens becomes involved in the development of national maturity and progress.

Lucrecia R. Kasilag (Former Director of the Arts and Humanities Center)—Passed away.

L.R. Kasilag (✉)
Philippine Women's University, Manila, Philippines

© Springer Nature Singapore Pte Ltd. 2017
O.S. Tan et al. (eds.), *Global Voices in Education*,
DOI 10.1007/978-981-10-3539-5_3

At this point, a summary of the Philippine experience in the development of music education in the country would be helpful in understanding the status of music education in the Philippines. In the perspective of time, the development of Philippine music has grown along parallel lines of the political upheaval in our country's growth as a nation.

Dating back from the Shri Visayan influence in the 13th century, waves of Indo-Malayans migrated into the country, long before the Spanish conquest of the Philippines in the early 16th century. Upon arrival, the Spanish colonizers found a distinct culture practiced by the natives. When Christianity and European education were transplanted by the soldiers and the friars into the Philippines, named after King Philip II of Spain, the native cultural vestiges were almost obliterated in the process of religious conversion for nearly four centuries. With the arrival of the American conquerors in the late 19th century, democracy and public school education were introduced and adopted. American jazz was easily assimilated by the Filipinos. Local composers wrote popular music in the jazz idiom which became the prevailing cultural output of the time to such an extent that U.S. Congress eventually passed a law creating the University of the Philippines (U.P.) Conservatory of Music in 1916, for the study of serious classical music, patterned after American music curriculum. Public school music and the singing of foreign folk songs and native folk songs as well formed the bulk of music instruction. Throughout the Commonwealth period in the thirties, and up to the outbreak of World War II, talented Filipino composers were sent to America for advanced studies toward the masters and doctoral degrees. Prominent among them were Francisco Santiago and Nicanor Abelardo who came back to the state conservatory and shared their compositional techniques and skills in the handling of music courses. Dr. Alexander Lippay of the Vienna Academy of Music brought European faculty and know-how to the state conservatory during his term as director in the 1930s. Dr Francisco Santiago succeeded him as the first Filipino director of the conservatory who served until war broke out in 1942. Meanwhile Lippay founded the Manila Symphony Orchestra, the oldest in the country, and established the Manila Music Academy, a private institution which raised fine graduates and performing artists.

Another leading music school was established by the German Benedictine nuns headed by Sr. Baptista Battig, O.S.B., who founded the music department of St. Scholastica's College in 1908. Its many outstanding graduates were soon to head music schools all over the country.

Soon after the war of liberation from the three year Japanese Occupation of the Philippines, there was a big increase in the number of music schools from the pre-war 12–33. During the Japanese Occupation, the U.P. Conservatory of Music was closed, being then occupied by the Japanese authorities. Dean Felicing Tirana established the Philippine Conservatory of Music at the Philippine Women's University, with many of the U.P. faculty in the teaching roster of the new school. However, because of the ensuing Japanese/American war in 1943–44, the Philippine Women's University was destroyed and everybody evacuated to the provinces during the burning of Manila.

At present, besides the re-opened state conservatory, private music schools offer the bachelor of music courses at the St. Scholastica's College, Philippine Women's University, University of Santo Tomas, Centro Escolar University, Silliman University, Asian Institute for Liturgy and Music, Santa Isabel College and others, under the supervision of the Department of Education. The Master of Music degrees are given by the U.P. Conservatory of Music (now U.P. College of Music), Philippine Women's University, University of Santo Tomas and Centro Escolar University.

Hundreds of gifted music teachers and young performing artists have gone abroad for advanced studies and masters and doctoral degrees in America, Germany, England, France, Spain, Austria, Italy and Russia. Volunteer music organizations have been formed, among them in 1956, the League of Filipino Composers and the Philippine Music Educators Group. Annual music education conferences attended by provincial delegates were organized by the Educators' Group with the cooperation of the Department of Education.

The U.P. College of Music and the Philippine Women's University (PWU) have led the pace in documenting and teaching Philippine indigenous music from the pre-hispanic times to the traditional and contemporary periods. The Philippine Women's University houses the Bayanihan Folk Arts Center and its internationally known Bayanihan Philippine Dance Company which has gone on several world tours showing glimpses of Philippine culture through folk music and dance raised to theater level. The PWU also has more than 500 ethnic instruments of the Philippines and Asia in its living museum which are utilized by its faculty and students at campus and off-campus recitals and lecture demonstrations.

In 1966, the Philippine Republic Act No. 4723 known as the Music Law required music as a formal subject in the elementary and high school levels with an annual appropriation of ₱500,000 (US$50,000 at the prevailing rate of exchange), for the proper implementation of this law. The University of the Philippines and the Bureau of Public Schools in 1968 undertook a "crash" teacher-training project, subsidizing 40 public school teachers who were granted leave of absence for one year to study at the University of the Philippines, the government providing tuition, books, living and travelling expenses. This Music Law existed for about ten years.

In addition to the state university, music teacher-training courses were undertaken by private conservatories and music schools. Enterprising music educators published their own textbooks with structured lessons based on European and American classical forms, including Philippine folk songs and the traditional hispanic-derived kundiman love song. The rondalla plucked string band of Spanish heritage has become the basic means of instruction and school music-making. The Divisions of City Schools of Manila and Quezon City hold regular annual rondalla contests to promote the growth of the rondalla. The native bamboo flute, ukelele and flute recorder are used in schools. Because of the prohibitive costs of importing foreign orchestral and band instruments, music teachers are left to their own resources in using locally produced instruments for the classroom. Pianos are at a premium at public schools.

The Department of Education, Culture and Sports (now expanded) holds yearly national seminars to upgrade teacher-training with delegates from the provincial regions during the summer months of April and May. Music experts are invited to share their know-how and skills during these seminars and workshops.

Succeeding the Philippine Music Educators Group, the Philippine Society for Music Education (PSME) was founded in 1971 at the encouragement of Prof. Frank Callaway, then president of the UNESCO International Music Council and the International Society for Music Education. The PSME has become to this day the principal music educators' organization to upgrade the teaching competencies of music teachers. It would be good to recall here that Prof. Frank Callaway and I were both invited by the Vice-Chancellor of the University of Singapore in January 1971 to prepare a music curriculum in formal music courses for the university. We had a fine opportunity to meet with the music educators of Singapore then.

In recent years, however, due to other priorities and financial cut-backs, space limitations and the lack of music specialists to handle music instruction in the public school system, music has been integrated with physical education, vocational arts, health and scouting. Such a superficial approach leads to nowhere, to be sure, in the acquisition of musical skills beyond mere body movements and rote singing of tunes. Hence, the very function and educative value of music as a soul filling experience, as a means of aesthetic and spiritual refinement and intellectual discipline are left unachieved. A serious realistic review of this matter has been on the board for some time now with the authorities and the music leaders with the PSME taking a firm stand for the restoration of music as a regular subject in the elementary and secondary schools.

An unprecedented and tremendous cultural renaissance has swept the country since 1969 with the founding and inauguration of the Cultural Centre of the Philippines (CCP), now twenty years old. Built by the former First Lady, Imelda Romualdez Marcos, the CCP has served as a cultural repository and a showcase for the Filipino artist, a vital link between the past, present and the future. The CCP has become a catalysing factor and a lively beehive of cultural activity extending from the traditional to the contemporary/avant-garde in music and arts. The Centre has carried an ongoing programme of regular Philippine and international music and art festivals and has brought focus on the role of the arts in education and improving mankind through the enjoyment of beauty and the exaltation of the spirit.

An ancillary organization under CCP, the National Music Competitions for Young Artists (NAMCYA) was established in 1973 by Presidential Proclamation 1173 "in response to the imperative need to preserve, develop and promote Philippine Music as an art and as a handmaid of cultural development, and in recognition of the Filipino's innate love for music."

For the past sixteen years, NAMCYA has been principally instrumental in discovering major musical talents from all over the country. The project involves some 600,000 young musicians and trainers and administrators in selecting the best among them annually. Yearly competitions are held at divisional and regional levels from which first prize winners come to Manila to vie for national honours at the final competitions in the categories of choral performance, solo voice and instruments, family ensemble and chamber music, in both western art music and Philippine indigenous and folk music traditions. A non-profit, non-government institution, NAMCYA has survived and grown mainly through dedicated involvement of volunteers, mostly leaders of Philippine music, periodic assistance from local government and civic leaders, with annual subsidy from the CCP and the use of its facilities, and nationwide logistical assistance of the Department of Education, Culture and Sports serving as the backbone of its yearly operations.

This then, in effect, is the story of the Philippine experience in the growth of music education in the Philippines—an unfolding of the varied manifestations that reflect the multi-cultural aspects of our people and their aesthetic needs in our changing society and in our growth as a nation. We have come to the forefront in fostering Filipino consciousness of a distinct national art—healthy, humane and dynamic!

Acknowledgements There are instances where we have been unable to trace or contact the copyright holder. If notified, the publisher will be pleased to rectify any errors or omissions.

Author Biography

Dr. Lucrecia Kasilag is a leading Filipino composer, music educator, distinguished administrator and writer. After completing her studies Dr. Kasilag had to give up a performing career due to a congenital weakness in one hand. She taught at the University of the Philippines' Conservatory of Music. In 1949 she completed a Bachelor of Music degree and then attended the Eastman School of Music in Rochester, New York. In 1953 she was appointed Dean of the Philippines Women's University College of Music and Fine Arts. She holds international and national positions in the cultural world and has a long list of awards, honours and scholarships to her name. Dr. Kasilag has written over 250 musical compositions, ranging from folksongs to opera to orchestral works and has pioneered in the research and use of traditional Asian musical instruments, juxtaposed with western instruments in compositions of East/West flavor, many of which have been performed in Philippines and abroad. She was proclaimed National Artist for Music, 1989 by President C Aquino. She was Director of the Arts and Humanities Center of the Philippine Women's University. She never really retired and was composing up to the year before she died on August 16, 2008 at the age of 90 years.

Chapter 4
National Education and the Scientific Tradition

Gungwu Wang

I am greatly honoured to have been asked to give the Ruth Wong Lecture. Ruth Wong was an educationist whom I have long admired. We were colleagues briefly in Kuala Lumpur. But when I first heard of her, I was wooing my wife, and Margaret spoke of her with admiration as a great teacher in her secondary school. She knew but a little arithmetic having missed four years of schooling, but Ruth Wong taught mathematics so brilliantly that, within two years, the whole class passed Cambridge School Certificate mathematics with distinction. So there is a personal reason for me to be grateful to Ruth Wong for having taught my wife so well. Thus, my additional pleasure in being here today to give the Ruth Wong Memorial Lecture and Margaret joins me in paying tribute to a great teacher and a dedicated educationist.

The subject of my lecture, "National Education and the Scientific Tradition" has come about because I recall Ruth Wong's work for national education, first for Malaya, later Malaysia and then Singapore, and because her teaching of mathematics symbolises the key to modern science. It is this science education that has given us during the past century or so the universalist ideals that guide the idea of excellence in education. It has done much both in laying the foundation of national education and in enabling new generations of Asians to internalise the scientific standards that are considered to be applicable universally.

Education for groups of elites has long been available in most societies. Education for all, however, has come only during the 20th century, first in the developed countries and as an ideal for the rest. As for excellence, it is harder to agree on the criteria we need to judge this by. There is elite excellence, that is, quality for the very few, and there is, with different criteria of excellence, all-round quality education for the many. For the former, it can be said that brilliant indi-

G. Wang (✉)
East Asian Institute, National University of Singapore (NUS), Bukit Timah Campus,
Tower Block #06-01, Singapore 259770, Singapore
e-mail: eaiwgw@nus.edu.sg

© Springer Nature Singapore Pte Ltd. 2017
O.S. Tan et al. (eds.), *Global Voices in Education*,
DOI 10.1007/978-981-10-3539-5_4

37

viduals can be found in every country and the fact of having such people does not tell us much about a country. As for the latter, the quality all round, that is a major gauge of a country's development. It depends, of course, also on how much a country can afford, and how much it is willing to pay for education. We know it does need money to deliver good quality education to everyone. Only rich countries can provide access to consistently good educational facilities and working conditions for their teachers. Furthermore, they can attract brilliant individuals from the poorer countries to their centres of excellence and thus ensure that these centres remain excellent.

Since the end of the Cold War, there have been many efforts to define a new world order or new ways of explaining the world. For many, there is the "end of history" school of thought which trumpets the ultimate triumph of capitalism and liberal democracy. This view would expect the West to dominate. If the world were to be described as a pyramid, it would be the top third of the pyramid, with the United States seen by some as the top third of that. If so, an Asia-Pacific that includes the United States, and other "Western" extensions like Japan, Canada and Australasia, could look forward to being near the top because of the powerful pull of the Americans. That could also mean, however, the top third will dictate the standards of excellence to the rest.

An alternate view focuses on the "clash of civilisations" and offers quite a different perspective. The West is depicted as being on the defensive. The universalism that it claims to represent is no longer valid. Its civilisation (or civilisations if Samuel Huntington is right to count Eastern Europe and Latin America separately) has been challenged by at least two rivals, representing the Islamic and the East Asian "Confucian" civilisations, which may combine to end the past two centuries of Western dominance. If this is true, both the West and the potential enemies of Western dominance are to be found in the emerging Asia-Pacific region. Is the region, therefore, destined to be an arena for future conflict between the countries that are expected to represent the two opposing sides? National ideals of education, under such circumstances, are likely to be submerged to cope with the ensuing tensions. If such conflict is imminent, there would be no universal criteria of what is excellent and what is not.

There are, of course, more optimistic approaches that look at the world as ultimately human and therefore one diverse whole, whether it be seen as a universal civilisation, a global village, or a series of interlocking and interdependent regions. Thus, even when there is no obvious world order, the Asia-Pacific region could still be regarded as potentially one which overlaps with others through complex networks, but contributes to the overall integration of a one-world modern civilisation. Such approaches have recently been questioned. They are portrayed as naïve or impossible, or as illusory images used to hide the reality of Western dominance. Or, they may mislead Western civilisation to overreach itself and go the way of some earlier civilisations that had destroyed themselves by being over-ambitious and self-deluding. All the same, the positive and universalist approaches are far from obsolete and still deserve our attention if we are to speak of educational excellence.

The main reason why this is possible is because, underlying the claims of universalism for the past two centuries, the triumphs of modern science have indeed established a control over the imagination of peoples everywhere. Their impact on modern education, including national education in all kinds of countries and societies, is a truly remarkable development. It would be a mistake to treat the advances in science as a peculiar, even unique, Western achievement. It would also be wrong to regard these advances as something that can be detached from the modern West and their results accepted in each nation without the cultural baggage that made science possible in the first place. It would be difficult to point to examples of rapid progress in any Asian country during the past decades and not recognise how much they were the product of modern science and technology.

You will all be familiar with the origins of modern science in Renaissance Europe and the development of mathematical and experimental methods that followed. The great thinkers and scientists after Newton and Descartes, through Watt and Stevenson, Lavoisier and Pasteur, Darwin and Einstein, are too well known to detain us here. They deserve the world's admiration and their place in history is assured. The scientific tradition I want to talk about today, however, is not confined to them and their splendid contributions to humankind. What I want to concentrate on is the idea that modern science could only have come about with the cumulative help of earlier scientific traditions. These other traditions were found in several civilisations. I would emphasize that knowledge of these traditions is necessary for a balanced and rounded understanding of the value of science in Asia.

By these early traditions, I refer to the four better known ones of the Greeks, the Chinese, the Muslims and the Christians. Each of these enjoyed a period of flowering followed by withering and stagnation which left it unable to make the leap to modern science. The truly important question is not why none of these led to the growth of modern science; the marvel is how modern science emerged at all in Western Europe in the 17th century. But this is not the question I want to talk about today. What is important is that modern science did not spring up when it did **fully formed** and owing no debt to earlier achievements. The geniuses who brought us modern science belonged to cultures and societies that had been through many phases of scientific enquiry. Some cultures had run out of steam or ideas. In some cases, their talented scholars had been thwarted by powers beyond their control. Science was man-made. It could soar to the heavens because of human will; but it could be aborted, also because of human will.

The extraordinary achievements of the Greeks have been widely acknowledged because key parts of modern science have been traced back to their inspiration. Such recognition confirms that the origins of modern science owe much to an earlier tradition. Similarly, there have been arguments in favour of even earlier traditions of mathematics, astronomy, medicine and technology in Babylonia and Egypt, of which we can find echoes in the traditions of Hindu India and Greek science. When we say that these traditions shared some ideas in common which did not lead much further at the time, this does not denigrate the attainments of these ancient peoples. Their efforts did have cumulative effects on civilisational growth and their contributions should be given their rightful place.

The same can be said for the Chinese, the Muslims and the Christians. The Chinese had their own concerns with mathematics, astronomy and medicine. They received considerable stimulus from West and South Asia, but also developed their own methods, especially in certain areas of mathematics and technology. The Muslims and Christians could be placed together because they came from the same religious tradition and, for some time in the Middle Ages, had some attitudes towards science in common. The Muslims, however, appreciated Greek science earlier. At the height of their power, from the 9th to the 12th centuries, their mathematicians and astronomers were some of the most sophisticated of that age. But these men were expected to give precedence to their theological needs, and the theocratic states they lived in tended to confine their studies and discoveries to what served the faith and not beyond.

The medieval Christians, however, became active in scientific enquiry somewhat later, from the 12th to the 15th centuries, and extended their interest to a wider range of fields. Important help was received by the development of autonomous centres of learning during this period. Such institutions were given a small degree of legal protection for scholars to engage in enquiries over and above the concerns of the Church. These included areas like calculations about the stars and the planets, medicine, anatomy and alchemy. And, just prior to the astronomical breakthroughs of Copernicus and Galileo, several key universities had been pushing at the edges of knowledge with the assurance of a degree of patronage. What, however, was unacceptable to the Church was the revolutionary nature of what Copernicus discovered, which challenged some fundamental ideas the Church had grown up with.

For each of the four groups, its scientific tradition carried them only so far and did not lead to the scientific revolution which occurred in the 17th century. The reasons for that are complex. There were religious inhibitions about certain secular enquiries and these led to the intervention of theological or bureaucratic states. In some cases, it was lack of recognition, accompanied by contrary inducements to turn intellectual efforts towards moral, spiritual or more practical matters which deterred scientific enquiry. In other cases, there were actual prohibitions against the pursuit of certain sensitive questions in the eyes of clerics or political leaders. And not least, there were no clear economic incentives for discovery and invention, least of all the kinds of protection for free enquiry and property rights which would encourage scholars to share knowledge in order to speed up progress. Only by doing this could they accumulate their experiences for the benefit of later generations, thus enabling each generation to be better prepared to make further discoveries.

17th century Europe saw the coming together of many strands of scientific thinking, combined with economic and political conditions, which favoured the innovative and creative scholars who were able to take full advantage of them. It is essential for us to understand how that came about and remind ourselves of the circumstances which made modern science possible, made it universal, and thus capable of continued growth throughout the world. This is not enough. Although it is true that earlier scientific traditions were inhibited and met with too many obstacles to lead to the modern breakthrough, that is no reason for us to dismiss them as unworthy of our concern. On the contrary, it is time for us to pay careful attention to the earlier scientific traditions. Let me explain why.

Firstly, if we neglect the origins of modern science, we would fail to appreciate what a successful revolution that was. It would lead to us to take science for granted, to take even modernity for granted, and not understand how truly remarkable the human mind is. Secondly, only by reminding ourselves of the complex and positive factors in earlier traditions can we understand what roles they played and thus grasp the way modern progress has been made. By knowing the kinds of social conditions that either prevented advances in science or accelerated them, we can help to ensure that favourable conditions are maintained for future developments. And thirdly and not least, for those of us in Asia, it is vital that we do not see modern science as something that sprang out of Western Europe without any antecedents. The danger there is that we may therefore assume that there is nothing in other traditions that could be called scientific in any way, or had any-thing to do with the development of modern science. Such a view would close off our ability to appreciate how, all over Asia today, modern science is being studied successfully with relative ease, and how important it is that the modern scientific tradition not be cut off altogether from earlier knowledge traditions in this part of the world. Nothing can be gained by alienating the modern mind from its deep roots in earlier human achievements.

The education scene in Singapore is a useful one for me to elaborate these points further. It is a microcosm of Western and several Asian traditions. Its national education has made splendid progress in the teaching of science and technology and in adapting what is learnt to practical use. At the same time, it is conscious of the need to recall the links of its various communities to their cultural roots. What it has perhaps not done enough is to remind the younger generation that each of the cultures present here had an earlier scientific tradition that is relevant to their present responses to modern science. If this is done, there would be less danger of that science becoming scientism, some kind of alternate religion. For example, it is generally known how modern science came out of the traditions of many peoples, our students would realise that science is compatible with the ideas and institutions that give succour to our society's moral and spiritual needs.

Let me illustrate this further. The Muslims and the Christians may be aware that their traditions had made contributions to the recovery of Greek science, especially after the fall of Constantinople in 1452, and to the rapid development of new mathematical skills. Similarly, one might also note the contributions of Hindu scholarship to Muslim discoveries in mathematics, astronomy and medicine. As for the Chinese, most attention has been given to certain technologies which enabled modern science to flourish and spread, notably printing, the magnetic compass and the invention of gunpowder. This background of earlier discoveries and inventions is a valuable starting-point. It could serve to examine those scientific traditions which in themselves did not lead to modern science but, in combination and over long periods of time, enriched the intellectual environment that made modern science possible. From that broader understanding, there could come explanations as to how different individuals and peoples today are receiving the fruits of science and mastering the problems of modernity. The way they seek to transform their societies in part or in full and make scientific knowledge a part of their own modern heritage is itself one of the marvels of the 20th century.

I shall not try to cover all aspects of this fascinating story. Because of its dramatic impact on recent developments in Asia, the response of "Confucian" civilisation in China, Japan and Korea to the acquisition of the scientific method is of particular interest. And because three-quarters of the population in Singapore is of Chinese descent and can relate to that civilisation, I shall focus here on how some Chinese regarded that scientific tradition. The point to underline is that the Chinese experience of modern science this past century owes something to that tradition. It needs hardly to be said that a similar probing of the very different Hindu, Christian and Muslim earlier experiences with science would be equally illuminating.

For the past few decades, the advances in science in China have been very impressive. Many people now take for granted that Chinese people should be good in science because of the remarkable achievements of its ancient civilisation. But, because the inventions of China were not followed by modern science, there are others who have been surprised that, when presented eventually with the fruits of modern science, the Chinese took to the scientific method so readily.

During the 20th century, Chinese scientists rediscovered a scientific tradition for China. This was in the context of a multitude of contributions to scientific progress, the recognition that varieties of ancient or medieval science, pre-modern or proto-modern science, had flowed into the mighty river of modern science. This does not mean that Chinese civilisation could be described as a scientific one, but it allowed the Chinese to say that they were no less scientific than the West was before Galileo and Newton.

There are many Chinese equivalents for the word science in its broadest sense of "truth" or "knowledge", but none is related to the development of modern science. If we confine ourselves to science as a methodology, there was no word in the Chinese language that would describe that way of determining truth. The nearest phrase would be *gewu*, to discover everything we can about something. This was more a philosophical ideal, which was valuable to scholars who did their utmost to establish the accuracy of documents and empirical observations. It was particularly useful for dating and editing ancient texts, as well as for arriving at the precise meaning of words and concepts. But it was not applied to the practical skills that the Chinese acquired or to the technological advances which the Chinese made through the centuries.

That separation between *gewu* and Chinese technical ingenuity meant that technology was never recognised as a source of knowledge about more fundamental questions in life. Thus, when Chinese scholars first encountered the idea that Western wealth and power were the results of modern science, and grasped what scientific methods and research did to speed up the industrial revolution and remake the world, they thought that their own civilisation was deeply defective. Many then turned against their own traditions and cultivated an obsession with science that was close to getting religion, or least as a substitute for religion, what I mentioned earlier as scientism.

By the beginning of the 20th century, there was general acceptance among the Chinese intelligentsia that it was essential for China to master modern science. Their position was that mere technological imitation was not enough. They and their followers were convinced that China had to move quickly to a willingness to learn more from the West. What was not agreed upon was what to learn and how much to learn. This period of acceptance lasted from the turn of the century to the 1950s. It was one of intense debate followed by the hardening of positions, not so much about the importance of science as about the nature of Chinese society and civilisation. Just before the May Fourth Movement in 1919, most educated Chinese were still confident that the ethical principles which provided the foundations of Chinese civilisation were sound. Learning science to strengthen China was necessary but it was no threat to the core of that ancient and glorious civilisation. After 1920, following intense debates at many levels of Chinese society, the position was reversed. In order to save China, the narrow and outdated moral and political traditions had to be replaced by scientific thought and modern methodologies, even if this led to the discarding of most conventional wisdom.

This included the idea that Neo-Confucian ideas and practices were obstacles to progress. They needed thorough reform at the least, and for the revolutionaries, they were better thrown out altogether. But there was also a deep underlying contradiction in that position. The talk about national salvation stressed the need for more science and technology and a deeper understanding of the values which made science so effective and Western countries rich and powerful. At the same time, it also required a rejuvenation of the Chinese people, of their pride in national identity. This meant they could not deny their heritage of a once great civilisation.

Let me take a few examples from China and from this part of our region to illustrate this. In China, there was Yan Fu at the end of the 19th century. He had studied chemistry, physics and mathematics in England and then introduced not only the ideas of Darwin, Thomas Huxley, Herbert Spencer but also those of Adam Smith, Montesquieu and John Stuart Mill, and many others. Here was someone who knew the latest developments in Western science and the social sciences, but who believed that it could co-exist with the humanist and moral values of traditional Chinese culture. Others who learnt their science indirectly through Japan, notably Zhang Ping-lin and Liang Qichao, were equally influential in calling for a new spirit of scholarship. But they too thought that the scientific civilisation of the West could be complementary to the moral civilisation of China. In fact, after seeing what happened to Europe at the end of World War I, Liang Qichao went further and publicly denounced the materialistic civilisation that led to such destruction and slaughter.

Of their contemporaries in this part of the world, I might mention the examples of Gu Hongming, Lim Boon Keng and Wu Lien-teh. All three were men who had studied scientific subjects abroad but continued to appreciate the rich cultural heritage of China. Gu Hongming (1857–1928), was thoroughly soaked in a classical Scottish education, including a good grounding in science and mathematics that enabled him to get an engineering degree in Germany. He was a good example of a culturally deracinated overseas Chinese (in his case, descended from several generations of traders who had settled in Penang), whose scientific education led him back to classical Chinese culture. Despite his early training in the sciences, he argued strenuously against adopting 'the intensely materialistic civilisation of modern Europe'.

Lim Boon Keng (1869–1957) was from Singapore and would be better known to you. Also educated in Edinburgh, with the necessary scientific knowledge to enable him to become a medical practitioner, he had a brilliant career in Singapore before taking up the presidency of the University of Amoy in 1922. He was a moderniser who wanted his students to have a good science education. Nevertheless, he was convinced of the value of Confucianism and supported efforts to preserve that tradition. Unfortunately, he had the misfortune of being the target of one of the sharpest critics of the age, the famous writer Lu Xun, who mocked him for being an arch-conservative. Since Lu Xun's writings are much better known, Lim Boon Keng has gone down in history not as the keen supporter of science education that he actually was but as the diehard defender of a dying faith, a reputation which he did not deserve. On the contrary, it might well be said that what he did for Xiamen University was a lot more constructive than Lu Xun's calls to reject the past.

Wu Lien-teh (1879–1960) from Penang, like Lim Boon Keng, was another Queen's Scholar from the Straits Settlements. He studied medicine in Cambridge and became world famous as a plague fighter in China and a pioneer in medical research. That he was a modern scientist who turned his knowledge to very practical use no one can doubt. Less well-known was his contribution to the first modern study of the history of Chinese medicine. In the midst of his scientific research, he continued to pay close attention to the medical traditions of China. He was thus a pioneer also in China's efforts to consider that tradition as worthy to parallel the modern medicine that he so ably advanced. Till this day, the two traditions have remained close in China, and reminds us that the achievements of the past could be richly helpful in national education today.

There are, of course, many more examples of learned and influential men who had studied scientific subjects abroad and returned to China to warn against undervaluing the social and political underpinnings of Chinese civilisation. It is remarkable how they initiated a series of intellectual and academic debates about science and civilisation which led to great political and ideological passion. The debates coincided with a period of disunity and civil war and with desperate efforts by patriotic youth to forge a strong national movement to bring about the unification of China. Western ideas were sifted through in search of suitable formulas that would help solve China's problems. The scientists were in the forefront of the debates, notable the new American trained generation around the Science Society founded by Ren Hongjun, Ding Wenjiang and Zhu Kezhen. Together, they led the call for more and better science education in all Chinese universities.

Non-scientists were equally inspired. Two examples would suffice here. Chen Duxiu and Hu Shih were particularly influential and their lives are illustrative of the politicisation of the debate. Both of them had a strong classical education, but this did not stand in the way of their fervent wish to see science and democracy developed in China. Although they parted ways and Chen Duxiu was diverted by the revolutionary ideals of Marxism and communism, while Hu Shih remained the liberal humanist, they continued to support the spread of the scientific method into all aspects of learning and education. They both contributed to the excitement that led the young to say: Young China must be creative, socially responsible, and must adopt a scientific approach to everything!

One of them, the young philosopher Fung Yu-lan, asked the famous question, why did modern science not develop in China after the brilliant start of its civilisation? He wrote an article in 1922, while he was still studying at Columbia University, entitled 'Why China has no science—an interpretation of the history and consequences of Chinese philosophy'. He asked this in the context of his concern that the lack of science in China was the key reason why China was weak and backward.

The debates of the 1920s ended with victory for modern science against Chinese traditional values. Scientism won the day and science became sacred, something of a holy cow. This was a pyrrhic victory. The politicisation of science as a measure of everything progressive had appropriated the intellectual discourse about a subject that was much more complex, that is, the nature of traditional civilisation and how it could help rather than hinder the process of modernisation. Thereafter, everything that was opposed to the received traditions was seen as scientific and progressive. All else was backward. This view continued among the most active and aggressive polemicists into the 1930s and 1940s who, directly or indirectly, supported the view that only Marxism and the Chinese Communist Party embodied the scientific approach in its socialism and dialectical materialism. It was thereafter but an easy step to painting everything as either black or white. This was done by equating all that was scientific and progressive with Marxism-Leninism, and all that was reactionary, backward, feudal-traditional and unscientific with the government that was trying to crush the communists.

The politicised polarisation became uncritically accepted among most of the patriotic and the rebellious young during the 1930s and 1940s. One example of that is illuminating. Chen Li-fu's *Sheng chih yuan-li* (The Philosophy of Life) was one of the compulsory texts for first year university students in the 1940s. Chen, a former minister of education of the Nationalist government, was a mining engineer trained in the United States. He tried hard to marry modern scientific ideas and methods to what he considered was well worth preserving in Chinese civilisation. His book, which argued that there was no contradiction between tradition and science, and that Chinese civilisation was compatible with the development of a modern scientific country, was rejected because of his political background rather than the validity of the argument.

In short, for more than two decades, those who clamoured loudest for science as a basis for national education started with the premise that there had never been any science worth speaking of in Chinese civilisation. Even the defenders of that ancient civilisation who described the glories of its material culture and the intellectual brilliance and artistic genius of the Chinese people made no strong claims to its having had a scientific tradition of any kind.

As an historian, I am aware that traditional Chinese civilisation has been seen as having prevented its practical geniuses from progressing to modern science. That civilisation extolled a philosophy that was holistic and organic, one that placed great emphasis on the absolute authoritarianism of both the family and state systems. Severe limits were placed on knowledge transmission that made it virtually impossible for any knowledge collaboration, except among family members (or, among some tightly controlled guilds). Otherwise, all new knowledge that the state did not know about would have been suspect. If anyone had useful knowledge which they did not offer to the court, that would have been seen as either heterodox and therefore condemned, or dangerous and even treacherous.

In such a culture, anything like technology transfer in the modern sense would have been impossible. The examination-based bureaucracy looked down on the practical discoveries of artisans and craftsmen, and there was little chance of the kinds of interaction which induced the officials to be creative themselves. It is not surprising that, in such an environment, something that can be described as scientific inertia or stagnation developed.

During the past five decades, there has been a manifold increase in the number of Chinese texts and artefacts related to early science that scholars in and outside China had found and re-examined. Most of you would be familiar with the remarkable work of Joseph Needham and his colleagues. Needham's *Science and Civilisation in China,* now sixteen volumes published with several more to go, has put the subject on the map throughout the scientific world. And there were numerous Chinese scholars who made it possible for him to tell the world of China's earlier achievements. In the numerous texts that have been translated and interpreted, there are found solutions in mathematics, astronomical observations and calculations, the magnetic compass, agricultural tools and techniques, alchemical 'experiments', the discovery of gunpowder, the development of printing, mechanisms in the 'heavenly clock'. These were remarkable scientific discoveries by any standards. Many of these have been accepted to a greater or lesser extent as support for the idea that China might have been able to develop modern science if other circumstances had been more favourable.

This has led to many Chinese rediscovering their science. The question has aroused the interest of many scientists, philosophers and historians of science as well as sociologists of knowledge. The literature on this subject is large and still growing. Let me just mention a few examples. We still do not know enough about all facets of early science and the conceptual framework in which some scientific and technological developments had taken place. Despite this, what we do know shows the scientific mind at work. There may be doubts whether China ever had a science civilisation, but even the critics endorse the need to ask why all the achievements enumerated in recent studies, especially those I mentioned above, did not lead to modern science. They do think it useful to sift out the nuances in China's material culture so that we can better understand China's present response to modern science.

Scientists themselves, of course, do not always agree. For example, two physicists, both originally from China, totally disagree with each other about whether there had been any science in early China. The first is Qian Wenyuan, a physicist from the People's Republic of China. He does not share the Marxist assumptions about the 'universality of science' prior to Newtonian physics. He believes that the technical inventions of the Chinese did not add up to anything that is recognisable as science as we know it. The cultural inertia in Chinese civilisation totally inhibited the kind of experimentation, initiative and creativity that modern science needs.

In contrast, Chen Cheng-i, who left China as a young man and had been educated in Taiwan and the United States, holds a starkly different view. He argues that scientific thought in traditional China deserves much more careful research. While he stops short of claiming that China had a science civilisation before modern times, he does suggest that Qian's views are too Eurocentric, that he had not asked the right questions of the many sources used. Chen has therefore set out to prove that the ancient Chinese thought more scientifically than we have given them credit for. The contrast between the two scientists brings out the danger of defining science anachronistically or too narrowly. If it is done anachronistically, we could identify almost any rational argument as potentially scientific. If it is done too narrowly, then we could easily conclude that nothing deserves the name of science until the age of Galileo and Newton.

Some interesting research has also been done by sociologists and economic historians, including some who argue that the rise of capitalism and the bourgeois class formed a unique driving-force in the rapid advances in science and technology in the West. Without this capitalism, there would have been limits to what could be achieved. But technological ingenuity was not enough for either capitalism and the industrial revolution or the rise of modern science. Another study contrasts the legal and educational institutions of China and the Islamic world with those of the West. It points to the beginnings of legal protection for some universities of Western Europe long before Copernicus. Such protection against both Church and State was essential if independent inquiries were to be pursued. This was conceptually impossible in China even during the relatively tolerant Song dynasty, least of all during the much more restrictive Ming and Qing dynasties. And without such protection of the efforts of scientists to pursue their researches freely and fearlessly, modern science could not have been born.

The question remains: China produces some of the most talented scientists in the world, how could it do that if there had never been a scientific tradition in the past? We know that Chinese civilisation suffered immensely during the century of foreign threat, military defeat, and political decline from the middle of the 19th to the middle of the 20th century. After 1949, there has been a new confidence in Beijing that China was at last being guided by science and technical advancement. Many writings now speak of three or four thousand years of China's glorious scientific and cultural achievements. In itself, the boast is not significant. What makes it interesting is that, for most of the hundred years before 1949, Chinese scholars had thought the opposite. It is, therefore, probably no accident that there has been renewed interest in the earlier Chinese view about modern science, the idea of 'Chinese learning as foundation and Western learning for application' that was so cogently stated by Zhang Zhidong about a hundred years ago. This had put the emphasis on modern science offering new methods, or new means of mastering the secrets of advanced technology in order to gain national wealth and power. That approach would be compatible with many other scientific traditions, certainly with those of the Christians, the Hindus, the Muslims as well.

This brings me back to national education in the context of pre-modern scientific traditions. The Chinese example deserves attention. Their efforts to identify a scientific tradition and provide Chinese civilisation an added dimension that links it with the outside world have given young Chinese scientists new confidence that their world of science has a broad and distinguished pedigree. In today's world, national education must do more than prepare future generations by attending only to the present and the immediate past, or to the local and the neighbouring region. The nations of the West themselves are successful because they have recognised the contributions of history, including history well outside their own region, to their growth as representatives of a scientific civilisation. New nations in Asia should learn from that, especially when there are scientific traditions of their own to explore and bring into present stages of development.

If national education fails to include the sense of range and depth in several scientific traditions, I foresee at least two scenarios for societies in Asia that give great precedence to science, however understandable that may be. One, the universality of modern science in our education will strengthen the assumption that the Western heritage alone had brought it about. It will follow that all sense of the past, and in the end, of the future as well, would be dominated by that single worldview. Secondly, the impact of scientific knowledge that is regarded as outside the framework of the living cultures that still have moral and spiritual meaning is likely to produce an imperfect and partial learning of modern science. Given the tremendous potential for modern science to uplift standards of living and add to the quality of life, national education needs to give it full rein. But if that education did not appreciate that other cultures have scientific traditions, it will not integrate modern science with the rich moral and spiritual life which people do need and which the traditions provide. I do not know what Ruth Wong would say to these thoughts, but I imagine she would agree that any science education which fails to recognise that science, no less than modern society, has a distinguished past which we need to know about more fully, would be seriously incomplete.

Author Biography

Emeritus Professor Wang Gungwu is currently Chairman of the East Asian Institute, the Lee Kuan Yew School of Public Policy and the Institute of Southeast Asian Studies at NUS. He was conferred an Emeritus Professorship by the Australian National University, Canberra in 1988. An internationally renowned teacher, scholar and researcher, Professor Wang was born in Surabaya, Indonesia on 9 October 1930. He grew up in Ipoh, Malaysia. After completing secondary school in Anderson School in Ipoh, he furthered his study at the National Central University in Nanking,

China. He then studied History at the University of Malaya, Singapore where he received his Bachelor of Arts (1953) and Master's degree (1955). He obtained a Ph.D. in Chinese History from the School of Oriental and African Studies, University of London (1957). His brief stay in China in 1947 stimulated his life-long interest in Chinese history and the trajectory that the country would take.

Prof. Wang began his career at the University of Malaya, Singapore (1957–59) and then continued at the University of Malaya, Kuala Lumpur (1959–68) rising to become Dean of the Faculty of Arts and Professor of History. In 1968 he went to Canberra to take up the position of Professor of Far Eastern History in the Research School of Pacific and Asian Studies (RSPAS) at Australian National University (ANU) where he later served as Director of RSPAS. He was at the ANU until 1986. He served as Vice Chancellor of the University of Hong Kong from 1986 to the end of 1995. With his vision and support, this university established the Hong Kong University Foundation for Educational Development and Research the first foundation of its kind at the local tertiary education level, to foster stronger links with the community and enhance this university's capacity for teaching and research. After his retirement from Hong Kong in 1996, he was appointed Director of East Asian Institute (EAI) of National University of Singapore (NUS), (1997–2007). He was appointed University Professor in 2007 at NUS, the third person to receive the institution's highest academic appointment.

Professor Wang has received several awards during his illustrious career. He was awarded the Commander of the British Empire (CBE) by the governor David Wilson of Hong Kong in 1991. He received from the Government of Singapore, the Public Service Award in 2004 and the Public Service Star Award in 2008. In 2006 he was bestowed the Outstanding Service Award from the NUS for his dedication in establishing the EAI as a teaching research centre on contemporary China. His scholarly contributions earned him numerous Honorary Doctorates from various universities across the globe. He has also been invited on numerous occasions to deliver named lectures in prestigious university all over the world. He is the author of many books and articles which focus mainly on Chinese history. His latest publication *Renewal: The Chinese State and the New Global History* was in August 2013.

Chapter 5
Approaching the Next Millennium: Education at the Crossroads

Awang Had Salleh

I consider it a rare privilege and opportunity to deliver a lecture in honour and loving memory of someone that is personally known to me. It evokes a feeling of satisfaction, of awe and humility at the memory of sitting at the feet of a great teacher, counselor, mentor, dissertation supervisor, dean and leader, and above all, a great motivator. The late Professor Ruth H.K. Wong is very well known and fondly remembered for her invaluable contributions in the development of education in Singapore and Malaysia.

If I may reminisce for a minute. When I was small, I often imagined and wondered at the prospect of my being unable to find my way home in the event that I lost my way on earth that consisted of nothing but a desert that enveloped the whole face of the globe. Thank God, I said to myself, in reality, there were hills, mountains, rivers, big trees all of which served as landmarks to guide me home. What if I were in a boat alone in the middle of an ocean with nothing in view in the horizon? Thank God, I again said to myself, soon there might be islands emerging in the horizon; and, at night I could be guided by the Northern Stars! In the end, I convinced myself, I could still find my way home!

When I became more mature, studying at a university, I asked the same question, albeit in a different form. What was there to prevent the emergence of intellectual chaos and academic anarchy if there was absolute academic freedom in the world? After a while, I was assured at the conclusion that even in the world of ideas, we could find and locate landmarks that could guide us from straying into intellectual confusion and academic disorderliness. These landmarks have been in the form of scholars, teachers, academic authorities and intellectual giants. In my own personal intellectual and academic development, Ruth Wong has been one such remarkable

Awang Had Salleh—Passed away.

A.H. Salleh (✉)
Universiti Utara Malaysia, Changlun, Malaysia

© Springer Nature Singapore Pte Ltd. 2017
O.S. Tan et al. (eds.), *Global Voices in Education*,
DOI 10.1007/978-981-10-3539-5_5

landmark. With her guidance and counseling, I was able to find my way home from intellectual wilderness of the immature mind.

With that brief tribute to the late Professor Ruth H.K. Wong, it is my pleasure to share some thoughts with you on the subject of education. The topic that I have chosen for this lecture is *Approaching the Next Millennium: Education at the Crossroads.* It is my hope that the title does represent the concerns of both students and non-students of education alike. The phrase "next millennium" might hopefully be seen as reflective of the concern for the future, while the phrase "at the cross-roads" might hopefully be seen as a reflection of the concern for the present.

However, a word of caution is called for. Furthest from what I have in mind, is to attempt to speculate on what education will look like in the next millennium. It is an impossible task for me to do. Actually, we do not have to go far back into history to demonstrate our inability to foresee what is to come in a distant future. Just about two decades ago, no one ever thought possible that we can do some of the things that we are now capable of doing, and in the manner in which we are doing it. When Alvin Toffler put forward his idea of the coming of the Third Wave, we were quite impressed because of the soundness of his arguments backed by over-whelming facts and evidences, but it was only within the past decade or so that we could see for ourselves the stark reality that we have in fact begun to enter this third era of revolution in human civilization. That being the case, it would be pretentious on our part to claim that we can talk about education in the next millennium—a period of one thousand and two years, one month and six days from now, to be exact.

What then, you may want to know, will I be talking about? I shall be talking about the "now", i.e., the present, as we approach the next millennium. Given the ever increasing rate of change taking place in the past two decades, I think, it might make sense to talk about education in a short time frame of a decade from now. I shall attempt to talk about choices available to education, now that we are at the threshold of the new millennium.

Before proceeding to do that, let us look at the peculiarities of our time, in terms of education, in the global context.

It has been said that globalisation has been the direct consequence of the unprecedented advancement in communication technology including space tech-nology, transportation technology, and above all, computer technology. Globalisation has made the world—though not the earth—shrink. It has made time seem to tick ever increasingly faster, although it has not reduced the number of seconds that make up a minute and the number of minutes that make up the hour. The unprecedented advancement in satellite and computer technologies, has brought about information explosion that penetrates into all corners of the earth. Suddenly, we find ourselves holding a dual citizenship, as it were. While holding on dearly to our respective national citizenship status, we are now able to feel that we have reached the status of a citizen of the world by virtue of our familiarity with things and events occurring anywhere in the world.

In this so-called Knowledge Era, theoretically, everyone has unlimited access to information, knowledge and—hopefully—education; provided that one is aware of the existence and the availability of resources; provided that one does possess the information and knowledge acquisition technical know-how; provided that one is willing and motivated to so do; and provided that one is not deprived of opportunities to do so. It is against this backdrop that education has to find itself a new role in a new situation, however unfamiliar the new grounds may be.

First, let us look back to the last forty years or so the world over. The following seem evident. First, education has been a scarce commodity in that accessibility to it is open to fewer and fewer people as they move up the educational ladder, although the nature of the pyramid and its profile may not be the same for all nations. Second, for some countries with highly planned economy, the state decides as to who should receive what kind of education and where. Third, educational access and achievement depends to a large extent on family socioeconomic status and its sociocultural background. Fourth, the teacher is the knowledge authority in the classroom. Fifth, in almost all countries, educational opportunities for the poor and the less-privileged is a national concern; hence, the introduction of affirmative action in education in many countries. Sixth, most teaching-learning activities occur in specific places called classrooms, lecture rooms, lecture theatres, libraries, and laboratories.

All these are fast becoming outmoded. Given the information explosion, teachers' role as knowledge authority in the classroom will be changing to assume a new role—the role of knowledge resource managers and learning counselors, facilitators and coordinators, as well as motivators.

The concept of teaching-learning as a process will also change. There will be a reversal of the proportion or ratio of the two elements in it. It will now be much less of teaching and much more of learning. What this means is that the onus is more on the student to learn than on the teacher to teach. The learners will enjoy greater degree of autonomy in deciding what to learn, how much or to what level, and where and who to learn from.

Given the speed and spread of transmission by electronic means, teaching-learning activities may not necessarily be conducted in conventional designated places. Instead, they may take place in the homes of the learners and in their work places. While conventional teaching-learning places will still be known as "educational institutions" or "teaching institutions" the work places that promote learning for their work force are becoming known as "learning organisations".

By virtue of the ease with which information and knowledge are accessible to many learners, unrestricted by conventional designated teaching-learning venues, the accessibility pyramid to education will be crumpled and the monopoly of it will be broken down.

As for the notion that education will slot people into various job specifications depending on the paper qualifications that they have obtained via formal education, education of the new era promises to free people from over dependency upon formal paper qualifications which, for so long, have been regarded by many as signs of the end, or the termination of further learning. Examinations that have hitherto been assumed to be terminal, as far as learning activities go, will in the new era, be seen as reasons for further learning.

The states are no longer in a position to decide for students what to learn, where to learn, and up to what level. For students, there are always ways out of compulsion now. Wider choices are available to them. They can also decide to step out of the education system, prematurely though it may be, in order to enter the world of work, knowing fully well that opportunities will be there for them to step into the system at a later stage. Even if they cannot get back into the same formal national system, there are alternatives available to them in the private sector education, including distance learning or distance education facilities.

A report, published in 1972, entitled *Learning to be*, by the International Commission on the Development of Education, UNESCO, advocated a learning society, which was regarded then as less easy to achieve; but seems to be a more realistic goal to achieve now, given the state of the art in education technology at the present time.

One area of educational activities that was considered burdensome but necessary was the administration and management of education. Standardisation in the administration of education was necessary in order to streamline the activities and make the system transparent. However, it has been very taxing on the system itself. Headmasters and senior assistants had to give priority to administrative chores at the expense of their more important and crucial role of providing curricular and teaching–learning leadership and guidance. Now that schools are equipped with computer facilities for administration, the administrative chores of school heads become drastically reduced, and they should have more time to give attention to the teaching-learning process in their schools. A number of ideal educational practices in schools could not be implemented due to other factors as well, such as space limitation, oversized classes, etc. Let us look at one example of an ideal practice that could not be implemented. While it is generally true that—other things held constant—students with high intelligence will perform more or less equally well in all school subjects, it is also true that factors other than intelligence make them like some subjects better that others, resulting in them displaying different profiles of achievement within a range of subjects. In such a case, it would make sense to make students join different classes for different subjects according to their level of performance in those subjects. An under-achiever in a particular subject, for example, should move out to join another class, one standard below, when it comes to a subject he is weak in; and by the same token, an over-achiever should be allowed to move out to another class, one standard above, when it comes to the subject he is stronger in. This would imply that, at the sound of the bell marking the end of one period and the beginning of another, students move out of their classes to join another class, either one standard below or one standard above their "home" class, depending on their level of performance in individual subjects. This should be an ideal state, but heads of schools dare not put it into practice for fear of chaos and indiscipline occurring along the corridors every time the bell goes off. However, this is now made possible through learning in classrooms that are equipped with individual student's computer stations so that students are able to shift to classes befitting their capabilities, without having to physically leave their classrooms.

Another area of educational activity that causes headaches to school administrators is the administration of examinations. Foremost in the minds of the administrators of examinations is the concern about the probability of some students copying other students' answers during an examination. The practice has been to employ invigilators in sufficient numbers to supervise examinations and watch each candidate with great suspicion. Standard distance from desk to desk of candidates is strictly observed so as to prevent a candidate attempting to read the neighbour's answers.

Thanks to modem technology, candidates may sit shoulder-to-shoulder without opportunities for copying since different sets of questions will appear on different computer screens. Examinations can now be held in smaller rooms deploying smaller number of invigilators.

Thus we see what was not possible some twenty years ago has now become possible, and with a greater degree of ease as well. All these are choices available to education. They are quite straightforward. They do not pose any theoretical or philosophical problems for implementation. The deciding factor in this case is actually funding.

However, there are other issues that are not that straightforward. These other issues must be seen in political, moral, religious, and philosophical perspectives. I would like to comment on just four of these broader issues.

Firstly the issue of DEMOCRATISATION OF EDUCATION.

This issue is contradictory in nature. Information Technology (IT) has flattened the pyramid in terms of learners' vertical accessibility to education. It is true that more and more people can further their study in the privacy of their home, and at their own pace that they individually set for themselves. They may choose to take a longer time to complete whatever education programme they want to pursue, but they are in no way denied the learning opportunity simply because they have to work to support their family or simply because they have to work at sea for part of the month and on the mainland for the remaining part of the month. In this sense, democratization of access to education refers to the removal of the handicap for those who are willing, able and financially capable to pursue further education. But how about those who are willing and able but financially incapable? Here is a case where distribution of educational opportunities may not be that democratic after all.

Another angle through which we could look at this issue is from the standpoint of accessibility to IT. Accessibility to information and knowledge presumes accessibility to IT tools. Those not in possession of the necessary basic IT tools will not have easy access to information and knowledge and are, thus, denied equal opportunity. Here, again, while IT liberates some learners, it delimits some other learners. Democracy is again put into question. A clarification is quite in order here. IT, just like other forms of technology—weaponry technology included—is, by its very nature, neutral. It is the political position a society or a nation takes vis-a-vis its IT policy that makes it democratic or otherwise.

It is, therefore, quite true to say that what IT does is to open up opportunity to learn to greater numbers of people. In that sense, IT democratises educational opportunities; but then, for those who do not own nor have access to the tools, IT deprives them of the opportunity. IT, in this respect, is discriminatory by being selective through default.

The solution to this problem should not, and must not, be by way of preventing the nation's populace possessing IT. This is a totalitarianism of the worst kind since all that such policy will achieve is mediocrity through retardation of learning capacity and capability of the nation. The formula should not, and must not be by way of pulling down the standards in order to cater for those below standards; but, should and must, instead, be to raise the standards of those below par to the level of the national norm. How this could be done, depends on the national IT policy referred to earlier.

Secondly the issue of LEARNING AUTONOMY.

Enhancement of learning autonomy enjoyed by the learners these days, is another impact that IT has brought to bear upon education. How does this relate to learners? Why should this be of concern to educators? Well, as all of us are fully aware, one of the major functions of education is to socialise the learners, especially the young ones, into becoming effective and useful citizens. This function has been carried out by educators through a balanced curriculum package. Students follow this curriculum package in the national system because they will eventually sit for national examinations in which composition of subjects to be taken by individual candidates must fulfill certain requisite, the purpose of which is to make students take those subjects that can inculcate in them positive moral, philosophical, religious, civic, humane, national and political values considered essential for the promotion of national integration and cohesion, national pride and identity as well as for the promotion of balanced and sound development of individuals—both physical and spiritual.

All this is possible only for as long as there is such a balanced national curriculum package that students are compelled to take. The issue before us is to resolve the question of the extent to which learners' learning autonomy is made absolute? If it is to be absolute, what are the necessary measures to introduce so that the learners are not deprived of exposure to "values" education through default.

Another related issue is the value of experiential learning through social intermingling among students within the confine of schools and colleges. Given that, hypothetically, students are allowed a full autonomy to choose what to learn and where to learn it, it is conceivable that there may be students who choose subjects to learn based on the immediate economic utilitarian benefit that they will get from them, and, at the same time, they may also choose to study at home by accessing their teachers through remote electronic means. In such a situation, are we not, then, encouraging students to become alienated from the mainstream political and social values of their nation?

Thirdly the issue of BROAD-BASED OR MULTIPLE LITERACY.

Further to the hypothesis that, in the future, there is an absolute autonomy for students to be selective in their choice of subjects to study, and given the increasing tendency for people to be technology-driven in their learning preferences, is there not a strong likelihood for the majority of people to be illiterate in arts, humanities, culture, history, and philosophy, although they will be highly literate in mathematics, technology, sciences and IT?

Literacy, in most dictionaries, is defined as ability to read and write. At the time, when I was a student teacher in the fifties, we were told that one of the functions of elementary education was to promote the Three R's, meaning *Reading, 'Riting,* and *'Rithmetic.* At about the same time, in the context of the rural adult education movement, the mission of the movement was to eradicate illiteracy in elementary reading, writing and arithmetic. UNESCO later extended the function of adult education in developing countries to include the promotion of what was called *functional literacy.*

The concept of literacy continues to undergo changes. In the sixties, it was suggested that education should promote the Three C's, meaning *literacy* in its traditional sense of the ability to read and write, *numeracy,* meaning ability to handle arithmetical skills, and *culturacy,* meaning, the ability to understand and appreciate cultural values in community or social life. For the first time, culture was recognised as an essential element in social life of a community.

With the advent of computer and information technology, another "cy" was added to the list making it a list of Four "'C's" comprising *literacy, numeracy, culturacy and computeracy.*

In the United States, about ten years ago, Hirsch Jr. shook the intellectual world of America with his book entitled *Cultural Literacy* in which he maintains that most Americans are ignorant about their own country, its history, literature and culture. Thus, we see that there is a gradual shift in meaning and emphases of the concept of educational function.

My own hunch is that *cultural literacy* will undergo further shifts in meaning. This shift is made necessary by the changing pattern of human travel and communication. In the present age of jet-setting, businessmen, corporate and political leaders, international students, artistes, sportsmen and sportswomen, academics and tourists, in the context of globalisation, coupled with the observations that as our world gets smaller, incidence of cultural, religious and political conflicts seem to be on the increase, it is imperative, then, that education must play a more crucial role of promoting *intercultural literacy* or *multicultural literacy.*

I was once struck by a caricature that I happened to come across by chance. I was struck by the simple message it conveyed. Two creatures from the outer space shook their heads in sympathy at a golfer who was struggling to hit the golf ball out of a trough. The golfer jumped up and down in great excitement when the ball went straight into the hole. That was the time when the two Martians could no longer bear to see the continuing suffering of the golfer jumping up and down in what they thought was a tantrum in an attempt to let out frustration. They quickly got into their spaceship leaving the scene feeling very sorry for the golfer. I thought that was a very good demonstration of a conflict of values in an intercultural—or rather, interplanetary—setting.

Another anecdote conveying a similar message is one about an enthusiastic American businessman who decided to take the next flight out of Narita International Airport back to New York, to report to the board of directors of his company, what he considered to be the good news; mistakenly thinking and assuming that his Japanese counterpart's nodding of head meant a total agreement with him, only to be told later that in Japanese culture nodding is more a gesture of respect, whereas decisions could take time to reach in a system where consensus building within a company is a rather elaborate process. Here again, a manifestation of value differences between cultures.

If, some time in the near future, history proves John Nisbait right in his prediction or speculation that as the world becomes more and more internationalised, there will emerge countervailing forces pushing towards a phenomenon that he calls *tribalism*, then I become more convinced that education must prepare students for intercultural and multicultural literacy that is so important in reducing tensions between peoples, religions, cultures, ideologies, nations and regions in our mission to promote peaceful coexistence on this planet earth of ours.

The challenge before us in education, then, is to find a sound and effective methodology for multidimensional cultural literacy despite the fact that IT may stand in the way.

Fourthly the issue of ABILITY TO HANDLE AND PROCESS INFORMATION.

Globalisation in respect of instantaneity with which information travels throughout the globe has revived and strengthened the fear, prevalent in the seventies and eighties, that mass communication travels one-way from the north to the south, from the developed to the developing world. People of the south are recipients of the influx of information that are very often biased and manipulatable.

I have been advocating that in the teaching of languages in schools, we should include the art of checking or validating the truth of pieces of information that we receive. The aim is to educate the populace to be smart readers of newspapers and magazines, smart listeners to talks, speeches and radios, and smart viewers of television and internets over computer screens, so that it becomes habitual for them to raise questions in their critical assessment of the validity and reliability of information they are bombarded with from the media, especially western media.

In conclusion the impact of change on our life in this Information and Knowledge Era is overwhelming. Education will have everything to gain and nothing to lose if it takes advantage of the new possibilities of IT when translated into ET (educational technology) applications.

However, education must also be proactive in its handling of the unintended outcomes, consequential upon indiscriminate and *laissez-faire* use and applications of IT in education.

I would like to conclude this lecture by making the following remarks. First, you may want to ask why, contrary to conventional academic practices, I chose to omit defining the topic of this talk at the outset. I do not know. I suppose the thought simply did not cross my mind then. However, despite the omission, the deliberation in the last one hour, inadequate though it may be, has shed some light as to what I meant by *Education at the Crossroads.*

Second, in the course of this lecture, I have wondered rather aimlessly at least at the beginning, but towards the end, I thought, I might have succeeded in finding my way home, as it were. If you share that perception, then, it is a fitting tribute to my teacher, the late Ruth H.K. Wong, who taught me to find a way home, once entrapped in the intellectual wilderness.

Mr. Chairman, ladies and gentlemen.

I thank you.

Acknowledgements   There are instances where we have been unable to trace or contact the copyright holder. If notified, the publisher will be pleased to rectify any errors or omissions.

Author Biography

Professor Tan Sri Dr. Awang Had Salleh, Emeritus Professor, Universiti Utara Malaysia was born on 24 June 1934 in Kampung Bagan Pulau Bentong, Pulau Pinang, Malaya. He was trained initially as an elementary school teacher at the Sultan Idris Training Colege from 1951 to 1954 and later as a secondary language teacher at the Language Institute in 1958. He obtained his Bachelor of Arts (Honours) degree in 1964 and a Masters degree in Education in 1967 from the University of Malaya. In 1969 he attended the Stanford University California, USA where he obtained his doctorate in Education and Sociology. His teaching career included being an elementary school then secondary school teacher, an assistant lecturer at the Day Training Centre, Malaya (1959–1961), lecturer at the Language Institute, associate professor and professor at the Faculty of Education, University of Malaya (1967–1978). Tan Sri Awang's administrative experience in educational administration included being Dean, Faculty of Education, University of Malaya (1974–1975) and Deputy Vice-Chancellor University of Malaya (1975–1978). He was Director (1978–1980), Mara Institute of Technology which became the Mara Institute of Technology University (UTM), Vice-Chancellor (1980–1984) National University of Malaysia (UKM) and the Foundation Vice Chancellor of Universiti Utara Malaysia (UUM) 1985–1989. After he retired he was involved with numerous institutions among which he was Special Advisor to the Ministry of Education, Malaysia (1989–1991) and Member, Executive Board of UNESCO, (1989–1991), Chairman of the Board, Sultan Idris Education University and in 1999 he became Pro-Chancellor of the same University. Actively providing leadership in his professional field, Tan Sri Awang has served as President, Malaysia Association for Education, President, Persatuan Suluh Budiman, and Chairman, Malaysia National Committee for the United World Colleges. He sat on various boards in both the public and private sectors.

He is the author of many books, articles and papers which focused on education, language and culture. In addition to academic publication he also produced poems, novels, short stories, plays and a novel in Malay. In appreciation of his services he received many awards; the Johan Mangku

Negara (JMN) in 1975, the Dato' Setia DiRaja Kedah (DSDK) in 1978 and the Panglima Setia Mahkota (PSM) which carries the title of Tan Sri in 1982. Amongst his academic awards: he was made Honorary Fellow ABE, United Kingdom in 1983, the Honorary Doctor of Law from the University of Brock, the Honorary Doctor of Letters from UKM and made Professor Emeritus of UUM. He was also conferred the Distinguished Fellow of ISIS Malaysia. He died in July 2013.

Chapter 6
Breaking the Cycle of Literacy Disadvantage in the 21st Century

Warwick Elley

I am deeply honoured to be invited to present the annual Ruth Wong Lecture for 1998. While I was never privileged to know Dr. Wong personally, I have read much of her work, thanks to my good friend Dr. Ho Wah Kam, and I find a great deal to admire in it. Indeed I share her dedication to educational research, and its role in informing policy; I share too her faith in the real benefits of schooling and her well-known enthusiasm for improving the quality of education in post-colonial societies.

I discover too, that by coincidence, she and I were both in North America in 1962, conducting our first experiments in programmed self-instruction, she in mathematics and I in learning theory. But I must not exaggerate our similarities. It is clear that Dr. Wong had many outstanding qualities that I could never hope to emulate, qualities that set her apart from other educators, qualities that made her a dynamic leader, that allowed her to challenge sacred cows, and to bring about real change for good. You do well to honour Dr. Wong and her contribution to excellence in education in Singapore.

I am delighted to be here also, because I have had many memorable intellectual experiences in Singapore, teaching at Regional English Language Centre (RELC), consulting with Dr. Tay Eng Soon and his Ministry staff, lecturing at NIE with Dr. Ho Wah Kam, and collaborating on the Reading and English Acquisition Programme (REAP) with Ng Seok Moi, Lysia Kee, Claudia Sullivan, Maureen Khoo, and the rest of the REAP team over a period of five years. While I am grateful for the opportunities I have had to consult with your educators, I must insist that I have gained as much as I have given.

In this address, I would like to outline the world literacy scene as I see it at the end of the second millennium. I will draw on two sets of figures, the adult literacy statistics that are reported annually for each country by UNESCO, and the findings

W. Elley (✉)
University of Canterbury, 12A Kiteroa Tce, Rothesay Bay, Auckland 0630, New Zealand
e-mail: val.warwickelley@iconz.co.nz

© Springer Nature Singapore Pte Ltd. 2017
O.S. Tan et al. (eds.), *Global Voices in Education*,
DOI 10.1007/978-981-10-3539-5_6

of the International Association for the Evaluation of Educational Achievement (IEA) international survey of reading of 9 and 14-year-olds in 32 nations, a survey that I had a large part in conducting and reporting (Elley 1992). Then I would like to draw some lessons from these surveys for the strategies that make a difference between the diverse reading programmes of these various countries and what does not. I would hope that these lessons might point a way to reducing the levels of illiteracy in the Third World.

Finally I will describe some of the studies that we have been conducting here and elsewhere of our attempts to raise the levels of literacy in primary schools where English is taught as a second language. This section will include a description of the local REAP Programme and I will argue that these studies are pointing a constructive way of breaking the cycle of literacy disadvantage that our large-scale surveys have identified.

UNESCO Statistics on Literacy Around the World

I should caution at the outset that UNESCO figures on literacy have been justifiably criticised for their lack of consistency of definition but I can assure you, as one who has spent many a day in the schools of Third World countries, that they are not wide off the mark. There is much validity in that stereotyped image of an underqualified, poorly educated teacher, struggling with a class of 50 or more restless pupils, seated on mud floors or three to a desk, in barren classrooms, with few or no textbooks. There may be a tiny blackboard, but there is usually a shortage of chalk and the pupils have little to write on. It is no wonder that children learn very slowly, and standards remain stubbornly low.

There are currently nearly 4 billion adults on the planet, and some 77% of them are classified as literate by UNESCO statistics. However the good news is that the figure of 77% literate has risen from 62% in 1970, and 70% in 1980. The reverse side of the coin is that the number of illiterates has changed very little as the world population continues to rise. The number of adults unable to read and write has been close to 950 million for some time. It is true too that 95% of these illiterates live in developing countries where most of the population growth will occur and nearly two-thirds of them are women, who are the mothers and grandmothers of the next generation.

Furthermore the funds allocated to schooling in most of these countries are miniscule compared with the expenditure on education in the developed world. Therefore, it seems that the cycle of disadvantage is generally predicted to continue. According to IEA statistics, the level of literacy at age 14 in a typical Third World system is 5 years behind that of a well-resourced First-World education system. It is clear, too, that girls who do attend school, read more and better than boys in nearly every country.

It is also worth pointing out that the correlation between women's level of education and the health and educational status of their children is positive and high. In fact, more schooling for the mother is associated with later marriage, smaller families, better nutrition, lower infant mortality, and higher status and influence in the community. There is a lesson here for many Third World governments struggling to meet their millennium targets.

Some of the difference between countries lies in society's attitudes to reading and the strength of their literacy traditions. According to literacy historians, some countries, notably Finland, Sweden and France have all had impressive levels of literacy for over a century, with no shortage of libraries, bookshops, newspapers and many well educated adult role models. Obviously, developing countries can do little to compensate for that.

One potentially encouraging sign in the UNESCO figures is that literacy levels in developing countries are considerably higher in the younger age groups than in those over 44 years. Clearly the efforts made to expand and improve education in recent years have paid off. Ironically, we find that it is usually the older generation that criticises the literacy of the young.

Cross-National Surveys of Literacy by IEA

Over the last 30 years, the International Association for the Evaluation of Educational Achievement (or IEA) has been conducting surveys of reading and other subjects in representative samples of students in member states in an effort to clarify the factors that might assist them to improve the levels of achievement in their schools In the most recent survey of Reading-Literacy (Elley 1992), 210,000 students aged 9 and 14 were assessed in 32 countries on common sets of reading tasks, using a variety of formats. The tasks were prepared and pilot tested by researchers in many countries and we selected them so that bias was minimised, and we agreed on which to include, during our regular meetings. The tests were administered to the students under standard conditions and the results converted to a common scale with a mean of 500 and a standard deviation of 100 at each grade level.

These results showed that Finland's students had the highest scores at each age level and in most subtests. At the 9-year age level they were followed by other western countries such as USA, Sweden, France, Italy and New Zealand. At the 14-year age level high scores were also shown by France, USA, Sweden and New Zealand. The developing countries did not fare well at either age level. Many of their students failed to score above chance level, meaning that they were virtually non-readers. On a question requiring students to fill in their personal details on a travel form, New Zealand students averaged 94% correct. Botswana 14 year-olds averaged only 34%. On a question requiring students to read and use a bus time-table, French students averaged 87% compared with 33% in Nigeria. Many more such examples could be given. The point is that although students in developed and developing countries are spending similar lengths of time in school, the outcomes of their education systems' efforts in teaching students to read are widely different.

After checking and correcting for indicators of small cultural or administrative differences, the researchers set themselves the important question of what lay behind these huge differences. Can we point to factors that will help us break into these cycles of disadvantage? It was obvious that the socio-economic differences between the nations contributed much. Therefore we developed a Composite Development Index based on official UNESCO statistics of economics, health and adult literacy in each participating country. This index showed a strong correlation (0.7–0.8) with the national mean reading scores of these countries. Thus students who are educated in a context where money is available to spend on schools, resources and teacher salaries, students and teachers are relatively healthy, newspapers and other reading materials are freely available and most adults can read, will have an advantage and produce higher outcomes.

To clarify further, we compared the highest and lowest countries on each variable we had assessed (through questionnaires), and reduced them all to a common scale to see which ones were correlated with the largest differences between the high and low scoring countries. The results for each significant variable were adjusted for their differences in socio-economic index (as indicated by the Composite Development Index) and are revealed in Table 6.1. We wanted to see which policies appeared to help nations produce good readers. The right hand column is a measure of how strong the factor is in differentiating between the high and low scoring nations.

It is clear from this table that a policy which enables more access to books is a critical factor in differentiating between school systems that produce the most good readers and the weakest such systems, when adjusted for the nations' socio-economic status. Thus systems which provide large school and classroom libraries and encourage students to borrow and read them frequently achieve the best results in reading tests. Of course, such a finding has to be interpreted sensibly. The books or reading materials need to be suitable for the children who have access to them and the teachers need to be skilled in finding ways of attracting the students to them. One other variable which showed a positive difference was 'more teacher reading to the class'—a variable that has much independent research support. A well-read suitable story does have much to commend it in attracting students to an interesting book and to the activity of reading as a source of pleasure.

There are numerous other sources of evidence about the virtues of access to good reading materials to support these findings in many countries, so we were not surprised by these results. Table 6.1 confirms also the importance of devoting more class time to the subject and of having a longer period of teacher training, as we would expect, and of having more female teachers. Of course, the results for the teaching of maths and science may be different in this respect.

More revealing, perhaps, were the factors that did not show up in Table 6.1 when adjusted for socio-economic status. Amongst these were class size, length of experience of their teachers, time with that class, frequency of evaluation of teachers and amount of homework, while the number of textbooks available was

Table 6.1 Selected factors that differentiated most clearly between high and low scoring countries, relative to their socio-economic status: (9 year-olds)

Education variable	Mean top countries	Mean low countries	Effect size
Large school library	3.50	2.06	0.82
Frequent silent reading	3.58	2.86	0.78
More instructional time	22.80	19.70	0.60
Large classroom library	55.10	43.50	0.51
Frequent reading tests	46.70	32.40	0.49
More female teachers	78.40	71.80	0.40
More years teacher training	13.90	13.20	0.40
More library borrowing	3.06	2.90	0.31
More teacher reading to class	2.59	2.30	2.30
More textbooks per student	1.66	1.57	0.19

positive but not significant. To improve in reading, the kinds of books that are written to attract children's interest appear to have more to offer in reading instruction than in many other subjects. In numerous other analyses we found, as expected, that the percentage of children whose mother tongue is different from that of the school are handicapped, although the results for Singapore are less severe than in many other nations.

The results of this type of analysis for the 14 year-old students was similar to those of the 9 year-olds although the amount of homework did show up as a strongly positive factor, and reading aloud to the class was less significant than in primary school.

Time does not permit me to reveal all the other findings of this enormous survey, but I have said enough to continue my story about breaking the cycle of disadvantage. As I had found in several smaller scale studies that access to high-interest books was a key factor in raising literacy levels, we began a series of studies designed to demonstrate to education officials in developing countries whether they could bring about large improvements in children's reading skills in deprived schools by shifting their resources towards providing a rich supply of good books. After all, most children enjoy a good story and might be prepared to use it as a basis for extending their knowledge of a language they are expected to master.

Fiji Book Flood

While working in the University of the South Pacific in Fiji during the 1980s, I teamed up with a local official in the Fiji Curriculum Centre and gained the cooperation of 12 small rural schools, with no libraries, to experiment with a flood of high-interest illustrated story books in English. The Ministry was sceptical about "wasting" their scarce resources this way. Therefore, we decided to go it alone. We raised $10,000 from a New Zealand telethon designed for good causes, and bought enough interesting children's books to provide a virtual flood of books (over 200) to the Grade 4 and 5 classrooms of eight of the twelve schools that agreed to participate. More than 500 children and 25 teachers participated in the project. In short one-day workshops, we trained the teachers of these classes how to use the books constructively every day to maximise their impact. We taught them how to implement the Shared Reading method. This method required the teachers to select a suitable story, talk about it, discuss the pictures, make predictions about what it would be about, then read it through aloud, stopping often to discuss the pictures and the text, and getting the children to read it aloud together. After further question and answer sessions they would do a variety of follow-up activities, such as drawing their favourite part, or acting it out, or re-writing it with different characters, or a different ending, and making it into a Big Book, for further sharing. Next day they might repeat these processes with a different activity. After three of four such sessions, the children gradually grow familiar with the story, its vocabulary and grammar and sentence structure, and are able to talk about it, use it to write new stories and the like. When such activities take place with a variety of stories over many months, the students appear to gradually acquire more and more language and the benefits are clearly demonstrated in relevant achievement tests and attitude scales.

Meanwhile the four "control group" schools that were not given extra books in the first year of the project, continued with their normal programme of daily language skills and drills in the text books of their Grade 4 and 5 classes (Tate 1967). They were also given a short workshop to improve their teaching of the methods and structures of that Tate linguistic programme. Before the project started, and after the first year, we administered a series of general English language tests to all the participants, including tests of reading, writing, speaking and listening, and measures of their attitudes. These assessments showed encouragingly large gains in all areas, so we decided to continue the project for another year. Would the improvements be sustained? We conducted another workshop for the teachers to compare notes and discuss their experiences before they carried on with the Shared Reading activities with different more challenging books as they moved up to Grades 5 and 6. At the end of the second year, the Grade 6 students all took the Fiji Ministry's Junior Examinations in all the main subjects. Once again, the results were very positive, especially in the English language tests showing that the book flood classes had typically more than doubled the rate of growth in their language skills, when compared with the control groups.

One easy way to illustrate the changes which had occurred is to compare the average stories which were written by the students on a series of pictures the children were asked to write about. In the Book Flood groups, the most common score (the mode) was 9 out of 10 marks, while the modal score for the control groups was only 2 out of 10. Here are a few typical introductory sentences written by students with those modal scores, selected from each group.

Book Flood Students

One day, Tomasi's mother was washing clothes beside the river, Tomasi's father was drinking yaqona under a shady tree.Tomasi was cooking the food beside their house, and his brother was carrying buckets of water.....
One morning when Luke's mother was washing, and the men were drinking yaqona, Luke was boiling the water...

For contrast, typical examples of the modal control group's sentences in the same exercise are given here.

Is there was the *women* in the tree, moth sitting in the tree, ther was a looking at his mother...
One day ther boy Seru is make the tea to drinking his morth was the colth...
One day morning their were a house, any village by the sea...

The gains made in vocabulary and sentence structure, by the children exposed to good books in this way are clearly seen in this contrast. Children who read and re-read high-interest story books mature rapidly in their command of English, while those who focus on skills and drills in language make very slow progress. In follow-up visits to the schools we found that teachers were very enthusiastic about the changes which had taken place in their students. They liked the books and their children's performance in the national exams was most impressive, jumping from a situation where very few of their students did well, to some of the best school averages in the nation.

Meanwhile, another book-based project in the Pacific was taking place in the small island of Niue. The Director of Education, Peter De'Ath, a New Zealand ex-reading adviser who was an enthusiast for Shared Reading, single-handedly wrote and produced a series of simple, interesting stories centred round the activities of Niuean children (De'Ath 1980). He believed that a series of meaningful stories, about families just like theirs, would provide a better basis for learning English as a second language, than the current skill-based Tate programme which was identical to that used in most Pacific Islands.

Peter called his Programme the Fiafia Programme. "Fiafia" in Niuean, means "fun". Using a similar approach to those of our Fiji Project, they introduced the new programme to almost every school and compared the progress made by his cohort with that of the previous year to evaluate the reading, the word recognition and the oral language of the children at the end of the year. I assisted him in the evaluation (Elley 1980). Just as in Fiji, Peter found rapid gains in reading in the book-based schools. This outcome was the first of many that we have found wherever we have used the Book Flood approach.

There is strong support here for the evidence of the IEA results that school systems which provide schools with good books and get the children to interact with them often, will bring about fast improvements in the target language for students learning in another language than their own.

The Reap Project in Singapore

My focus is on raising literacy levels around the world, but I must also address today the parallel project we conducted in Singapore. When I first came to Singapore in 1984 to conduct a training course at RELC, I was introduced to the Minister of Education who expressed some concern about the levels of English in primary schools here. He referred to a study conducted by the Singapore Institute of Education, which had demonstrated serious weaknesses in children's reading of English (Ng 1984). He asked if I had seen any examples of projects which appeared to raise the standards of English during my travels. I discussed the Fiji Book Flood and lent him a copy of my report on the project (Elley 1983).

He read it with interest and discussed it with others in his Ministry. Not long afterwards he announced that he wished to start a similar project across all aspects of English language in a pilot study in Singapore primary schools. I was asked to serve as the external consultant, and work with Dr. Ng Seok Moi, Lysia Kee and Claudia Sullivan and a team of other staff members in the Institute of Education, to help implement and evaluate it as it progressed.

After an extensive review of research and close observations of Singapore children in their English classrooms, the team designed a pilot study of 30 schools in which children in Years 1 to 3 would be exposed to a rich diet of interesting story books and study them using the Shared Reading and Language Experience Approach, suitably adapted for Singapore conditions. The project was referred to as the Reading and English Acquisition Project (REAP) (Kee 1984).

In 1985 the REAP Project was started in 30 primary schools. The Year 1 teachers received 60 illustrated story books for the Shared Reading lessons along with detailed guide notes on how to use them. The books were imported as we could find very few suitable books here in English at the time. Later on, 150 more books were provided when the children were ready for them. Teachers were given short workshops on the Shared Reading Approach along with guide books and some very good tape-slide demonstrations. Further workshops were given later on to help the teachers implement the Language Experience Approach which was not widely known here.

Next year we extended the project to Year 2 pupils in the same schools, and the following year (1987) to Year 3. Meanwhile at the end of each year the pupils in the 30 schools were given a wide range of English tests and their examination results also compared with those of control groups who did not receive extra books to work with. In 53 out of the 65 comparisons we made, we found significant differences favouring the experimental classes. Once again we had strong evidence that a diet of high-interest illustrated story books—and some non-fiction—had a measurable impact in raising children's reading and English levels, a promising sign for such a strategy in breaking down the cycle of disadvantage in all systems where children are learning in a language different from that of the home. Furthermore, we found that the teachers also showed considerable enthusiasm for this approach, after an initial period of scepticism for such a method of fun-filled activities.

Once the Ministry saw the results of our studies and the support given by the teachers, they extended the project to all primary schools with very impressive results in subsequent international surveys not only in reading studies, but also in the other subjects studied. As you will know, Singapore had by far the best results in the 1990 IEA study of 32 nations when compared with other countries where children were learning in their second language.

No doubt you have heard that the REAP team has also been involved in introducing a similar experiment in the schools of Brunei, with encouraging results so far. We have initiated other similar programmes in the primary schools of Sri Lanka and South Africa with very similar positive outcomes and are planning more studies in other developing countries in an effort to reduce the huge gaps between children in developed and developing countries.

There is therefore much to be said for a policy which exposes children to an abundance of interesting books and encourages them to follow their interests in reading them. It teaches the students new vocabulary and sentence structures, how to read and comprehend other worlds, how to visualise new possibilities, how to think beyond the square, and how to speak and write in more original and interesting ways. I hesitate to say that this is a magic bullet, but it is surely a strong and measurable way to show rapid improvements. I trust I have made my case.

Thank you.

References

De'Ath, P. R. T. (1980). The shared book experience and ESL. *Directions (USP, Fiji)*, 4, 13–32.
Elley, W. B. (1980). A comparison of content-interest and structuralist-reading programmes in Niue primary schools. *New Zealand Journal of Educational Studies, 15*(1), 39–53.
Elley, W.B. (1992). *How in the world do students read? IEA Study of Reading Literacy*. The Hague, Netherlands: International Association for the Evaluation of Educational Achievement (IEA).
Elley, W. B., & Mangubhai, F. (1983). The impact of reading on second language learning. *Reading Research Quarterly, 19*(1), 53–67.
Kee, L. (1984). *Concept paper on REAP*. Singapore: Ministry of Education.
Ng, S. M. (1984). Reading acquisition in Singapore. *Singapore Journal of Education, 6*(2), 15–19.
Tate, G. M. (1967). *Teaching structure: A teacher's handbook*. Wellington, Netherlands: A. H. and A. W. Reed.

Author Biography

Professor Warwick Elley is Emeritus Professor of Education, University of Canterbury. He was born and bred in Auckland and after teaching at primary and secondary levels in Auckland and Christchurch he left New Zealand in 1956 for England and later Canada to continue his studies and gain further teaching experience. He taught at high schools in London and Vancouver, chiefly in English and mathematics, and gained his Ph.D. in Edmonton, Alberta. Much of his research in universities in Canada, Auckland, Fiji and Canterbury and at the New Zealand Council for Educational Research has focused on assisting children with literacy problems and assisting their progress. From 1985 Warwick assisted the Singapore Ministry of Education to use the 'book flood' method in teaching English to the first three grades of primary school. Teachers were trained in the New Zealand Shared Reading and language Experience methods, and regular testing of the children showed that their reading and language skills improved with this type of tuition. The result is that the programme is used in all schools nationwide.

Warwick became the Chair of the International Association for the Evaluation of Educational Achievement (IEA) Reading and Literacy Survey which was conducted in 1990 and 1991, testing literacy in thirty two countries. In 1992 Warwick was awarded the International Reading Association's International Citation of Merit for his research on literacy. He has been acknowledged as a world leader in literacy research with a number of national and international awards. At the end of 1994 Professor Warwick Elley retired from his university post at the University of Canterbury. Since his retirement he has served as an international consultant on education assessment policies for the World Bank, International Reading Association, NZ Aid, and other agencies. He continues to write and is kept busy with international consultancy work.

Chapter 7
Education Administration: Analysis, New Challenges and Responses

Paul Min Phang Chang

Mr. Chairman, ladies and gentlemen. May I invite you to stand and join me in a short and silent prayer in memory of Dr. Ruth Wong. I am sure Dr. Ruth Wong in heaven is very pleased that our affection for her over the years remains undiminished.

Tribute to Dr. Ruth Wong

I am thankful for the honour and privilege accorded me to be your guest speaker this evening.

I accepted the invitation because it provides me an opportunity to pay a personal tribute to Dr. Ruth Wong whom my wife and I have always regarded with deep affection as our dear sister. Some of you may not have noticed that Dr. Ruth Wong and I were born in the same year, 1918, the year of peace that marked the end of the First World War.

When Dr. Ruth Wong was in Malaysia heading the Faculty of Education which she established, she and I worked closely together to develop quality teacher education. What impressed me most was her request that she be allowed to accompany me to visit Malay schools in remote areas, Chinese schools in new villages and Tamil schools in rubber estates in order to gain first-hand experience of problems which her students would have to face when posted to such schools after graduation. Her commitment to promote quality teacher education relevant to Malaysian school situations was total. I felt a sense of fulfilment when I managed to visit Dr. Ruth Wong in the hospital in Singapore. To me, it was a painful meeting

Paul Min Phang Chang (Former Visiting Professor of Education)—Passed away.

P.M.P. Chang (✉)
University of Armidale, Armidale, NSW, Australia

© Springer Nature Singapore Pte Ltd. 2017
O.S. Tan et al. (eds.), *Global Voices in Education*,
DOI 10.1007/978-981-10-3539-5_7

knowing full well that she was suffering from a very serious ailment. Her courage and her faith in Jesus Christ were an inspiration and transformed my painful feeling into a willing acceptance of the will of God. You will now appreciate the close ties that existed between me and Dr. Ruth Wong and how much I value this opportunity afforded me to meet members of Dr. Ruth Wong's family and some of her disciples in Singapore.

Reasons for Choice of Topic

Two reasons prompted me to choose education administration as the topic of my presentation. Firstly, this aspect of education has not been dealt with by any of the previous speakers of this series of Ruth Wong Memorial Lectures. The second and more important reason is that it is now recognized that education administration plays a crucial role in determining quality education.

Formal Teaching of Education Administration and Development of Theories

It was not until the nineteen-fifties that serious efforts began to be made initially in the U.S.A. to teach education administration formally and to develop relevant theories. Prominent among the pioneers are Andrew Halpin, D.E. Griffiths and J.W. Getzels.

In the mid-sixties, universities in the United Kingdom began to offer courses in education administration led by Professor George Baron of the Institute of Education, University of London and Professor William Taylor of Bristol University.

The man who introduced the study of education administration to Asia and the Pacific region is the late Professor William Walker. It was William Walker who founded the influential Journal of Education administration and established the Commonwealth Council for Education Administration. The Singapore Education Administration Society is an affiliate member of the Council. Another influential non-governmental professional body that organises every two years a symposium on different aspects of education administration in different countries in South East Asia and the Pacific Region is the South East Asia and the Pacific Region Education Administrators' and Managers' Symposium, founded in Malaysia in 1969. It will be celebrating its 30th anniversary in Taiwan in December this year. Singapore is represented on the Board of Directors of SEAPREAMS by Mrs Belinda Charles.

Since the nineteen-fifties there has been a massive increase in publication on the theory and practice of education administration. Yet, none of the theories have so far reflected adequately the numerous tasks to be fulfilled by practitioners. There is, however, one consensus that education administration is a very complex phenomenon or professional field of study.

Some Major Problems that Account for the Complexity of Education Administration

Leading the list is the enormous and increasing size of student population. More challenging than sheer numbers is the wide range of abilities and capacities that exist not only among students but also among teacher-trainees and even teachers.

All educators are aware of the varying abilities among students but not many are sensitive to the same problem that exists among student-teachers and teachers. In many countries teacher educators tend to teach their students as if they belong to a homogenous group. As a result, the standard of knowledge and skills acquired varies according to the abilities of the students. Some school principals do not realize that there are teachers who need more professional help and support than others because of differences in abilities. Constantly putting less competent teachers on the carpet is no solution to the problem. It will only increase the blood pressure of the school principals. Being able to transform a less competent teacher to be a competent teacher and a competent teacher to be a still better teacher is a very rewarding challenge to education administrators.

Complex Interaction

The second serious problem and challenge to education administrators is the very complex interaction involving students, teachers, school principals, members of boards of governors and of parent-teacher associations and bureaucrats.

Just two months ago, there occurred in Kuala Lumpur a massive demonstration by the entire student population and strike by teachers of an independent community-based Chinese secondary school. The demonstration and strike were sparked off by the chairman of the board of governors issuing a letter terminating the services of the school principal and demanding that she should leave the school premises within 24 h.

This is a clear case of problems stemming from complex interaction. It appears that there were conflicts of interest between members of the board of governors and the parent-teacher association. There was also disagreement on policy issues between the school principal and some members of the school governing board. Students and the teaching staff came out in full support of the school principal.

If only members of the school board of governors and of the parent-teacher association had some exposure to the principles of education administration, particularly theories of conflict mediation, such an unpleasant incidence would not have occurred.

Problems of Recruiting Quality Candidates to the Teaching Profession

In the past when employment opportunities were limited, there was no difficulty in recruiting bright students to the teaching profession. Today, education has to compete with the medical, legal, engineering, accounting and electronic professions, just to mention a few, to recruit quality candidates. These better paid professions can demand high entry qualifications as they are the priority choices of most bright students. Teacher training institutions have to be content with applicants with lower entry qualifications. There are exceptions but they are few and far between. In Australia, for example, entry to a medical school requires a minimum of 450 out of 500 points based on the results of the Higher School Certificate or its equivalent "A" level examination.

A depressing situation exists in certain countries where the brightest students, on completing their secondary education, are sent overseas on scholarships to further their studies. The bright ones gain easy access to local universities because a quota system operates in their favour. The less bright join the local technical colleges. The least bright end up training to be teachers!

Erosion of the Social Prestige of the Teaching Profession

Before the introduction of democratic, free and universal education, teachers were looked upon with high esteem because they were ranked among the best educated in the community. Teachers, then, were often sought by the illiterate to read and write letters. They were, in fact, the unofficial honorary scribes and consultants of small communities. Today, such services are no longer required. There are now not a few parents who are better educated and hold better professional qualifications than teachers. Some even have the arrogance to tell school principals how to manage schools. These same people, however, do not dare to trespass on the professional territories of doctors and lawyers. It is ironical that democratisation of education opportunities constitutes one of the factors that account for the erosion of the social prestige of teachers. This problem is serious and has to be addressed because it has an indirect influence on the recruitment of teachers.

Economic and Social Changes

Accelerated economic development creates better and more varied employment opportunities, better health care and other social services, better facilities for transportation and communication and better means of production. All these changes create new demands and new skills which education planners and administrators must take into account when formulating new learning objectives and restructuring curriculum.

Rapid economic development also generates a host of social problems such as materialism, consumerism, erosion of family values, drug addiction, and increase in juvenile crimes. Schools must pay more attention to the moral development of students. A telling example of infection of students with the social disease of materialism and consumerism is the tacit approval given to students to celebrate their end of school career in expensive hotels when they can ill afford to do so without financial help from their over indulgent parents. Why cannot school halls be used for such celebration? The use of school halls will provide students with opportunities to exercise their initiative and creativity, to decorate the school halls, organize the supply of food and beverages, and provide their own music and entertainment. We stress the need to teach students to develop initiative and creative skills and yet when opportunities arise, we stifle the exercise of such skills.

Explosion of Information Technology

At the moment it is difficult to predict the long-term impact of information technology on the development of education. Immediate benefits can be seen in the easy and rapid access to learning resources. Learning can now be self-directed and self-assessed, thus reducing to a certain extent the workload of teachers. Computers are definitely useful in simplifying the chores of administration, thereby enabling school principals to have more time to deal with professional matters.

Some teachers harbour concern and even fear that the increasing use of information technology will have a negative effect on their role and even further erode their professional status and social prestige. The fear is unfounded. There are certain skills no scientific technology can replace. Uppermost in my mind are oral communication and interpersonal-relationship skills that require interaction between two persons or more. Just as there is a difference between watching a live performance in a theatre and viewing the same on television or even on a big screen, there is a marked difference between listening to the exposition of an eloquent and spirited teacher and working individually with a lifeless computer. The passionate love of a teacher for his or her subject is highly infectious and can be a life-long inspiration to the students. It is reported in the September 1977 issue of *Asiaweek* that when we move into the next millennium information era, there will be a greater demand for teachers to provide a balanced education for information technologists.

Issues of Equity and Quality

This appears to be a perennial problem that defies complete solution.

Policy-makers, education planners and administrators have two options. To uphold the principle of equity, one option is to have limited human and financial resources distributed equally to all schools. This option is likely to result in the lowering of standards because, to cite a common saying: "the butter is spread too thinly over the slice of bread". The other option is to have more resources allocated to some specially selected schools to develop them as centres of excellence and to ensure that the interests of the talented is not sacrificed in the name of equality. These schools will become the cradles of future leaders of the country.

Ideally, every effort should be made to enable all schools to achieve a minimum of acceptable standards. In reality, in most developing countries, it is difficult to achieve the desirable balance.

Communist China provides a good example. There are 'key' schools and 'key' universities which are well endowed to produce the much needed future leaders for the country. Because of limited resources and the enormous size of student population, there exists vast disparity in standard between developed and less developed areas and between urban and rural schools. It is reported that in some very deprived villages, primary school teachers are so poorly paid, no girls will want to marry the male teachers.

Uncritical Acceptance of Foreign Models

It is always a gainful experience to visit institutions of learning in foreign countries to see how and what they do to achieve excellence in education. However, such visits must be made with a critical mind to evaluate that what works in one country may not work in another because of differences in culture and state of economic development.

Let Me Cite Three Examples

I read that a delegation of school principals were sent to the U.S.A. to visit schools which are noted for their innovative programmes. They came across an institution that had a programme to transform schools into learning organizations. My immediate reaction and the reaction of many of my friends is that if schools are not learning organizations, what are they? It is like wanting to transform men into human beings ...

Then, there is a programme that wants to transform schools into learning and thinking organizations, seemingly a step more advance than the first programme. If I may use a metaphor, it strikes me that one of the tripods is missing in this programme. Is it enough for students just to learn how to learn and think? In Malaysia, one serious problem confronting teachers at all levels is that students do not know how to apply what they have learnt.

Finally, a very disturbing so called innovation is attempts to redesignate school principals as chief executive officers (CEOs). Schools are not business organizations. The primary functions of schools are to develop the potentials of the individuals and to teach living skills. The Chinese summarise these two important functions into four characters: YU REN, YU CAI, which mean, *to educate an individual, and to impart skills*. Redesignating school principals as CEOs will destroy their distinctive professional identity. In Singapore, there are thousands of CEOs but there is only one dean of the school of education. I cannot imagine the dean will want to be addressed as CEO and lose his distinctive professional identity and get lost among so many CEOs. Models of education administrators are not Henry Ford, Bill Gates or George Soros. They are Jesus, Buddha, Prophet Mohammad, Confucius and Tagore. And in Singapore, Dr. Ruth Wong. Blind admiration and acceptance of foreign models will stifle creativity and undermine self-confidence.

This short list of eight problems and challenges can be further extended. However, they should be enough to throw some light, within the time constraint, on the complexity of education administration.

Centralised System of Education and Creative Management

Another major concern of my presentation is the assumption that there is no management in a centralised system of education.

Professor Nicolas De Witt of Indiana University, U.S.A. and UNESCO consultant, in his paper "Modern Approaches to School Administration and Management", presented at the 1972 Singapore National Seminar on Education Administration and Management, asserted that there is really no management of schools in a centralised system of education. He argued that in Singapore 'a school principal is not a decision maker but a decision taker'.

Most recently, in the early part of the year, Anthony Ang of Singapore, in his article titled "Ranking Schools by Industrial Models", published in the Singapore Straits Times, assumed that just because government plays key roles in funding and policy making, "no principal really needed to think about running a school any other way except to comply with the Ministry of Education's requirements".

I find it difficult to accept the two assumptions. I will prove that if we interpret education administration in terms of roles, each related to a specific task with its own set of theories, there is scope for creative management.

Nine major roles are identified and brief comments will be made on each. The nine major roles are: education administrator as (1) manager, (2) professional leader, (3) human relations facilitator, (4) transmitter of values, (5) change agent, (6) conflicts mediator, (7) finance controller, (8) evaluator and (9) philosopher.

Manager

Management is a continuing process that aims at maximising the use of available human, material and financial resources to achieve defined goals.

The process involves (1) formulation of operational objectives; (2) assessment of resources; (3) designing strategies to achieve objectives; (4) coordination; (5) decision-making; (6) communication; (7) implementation; (8) evaluation.

Education management may be described as the umbrella under which all the other roles subsume. It is also the vertical dimension of education administration with primary emphasis on technical management. There are almost endless numbers of theories on management. Selection for consultation must be made with a critical mind to ensure that they are applicable to local situation. Often, modification and adaptation are necessary.

Professional Leadership

This is a very crucial role. Many theorists equate effective management with effective leadership. Some of the important functions are:

1. To create a learning, thinking and action-oriented culture that favours continuing professional and personal development of teachers.
2. To motivate teachers to work as equal partners sharing common mission and total commitment. On no account must teachers be looked upon and made to feel as subordinates.
3. To win the confidence and trust of teachers, knowing each as an individual and not a functional unit;
4. To help to reduce stress and allow teachers to have time to read, reflect and share experience with one another.
5. To encourage teachers by personal example, to read widely reference books and professional journals. Books, journals and video tapes are tools that facilitate continuing professional development. Computers should be used extensively to seek required information.

Effective professional leadership is essential to achieve excellence in education.

Human Relations Facilitator

This is a very challenging role, vital to achieve quality education administration.

Some theorists also equate effective management with effective management of people.

Effective education administrators must be able to lead their staff to work successfully with different people in all situations, especially with those who hold strong opposite views.

Publications on human resource management and theories of managing people are worthwhile consulting.

Transmitter of Values

This is a difficult role because of conflicts between traditional and modern values and controversies between western and eastern values.

The main and important task is to teach students to discriminate positive from negative values irrespective of whether they are eastern or western, traditional or modern.

Values are best inculcated by personal examples, references to acceptable models and not so much by preaching. The transmission of values should be activities-oriented. Many schools in the United Kingdom and Australia require students before graduation to spend some time, ranging from a fortnight to a month working in hospitals, homes for the aged and handicapped, and people suffering from different physical disabilities. Such attachment allows students to gain first hand experience of problems facing less fortunate people.

An interesting project is one requiring students to work during school vacation over a period of three years to earn and save enough money to travel to a less developed country to work with the marginalised people. My granddaughter, who attended a private school in London, spent three weeks in Calcutta working with the nuns in Mother Teresa's Home.

It is doubtful whether religious or moral education should be taught as an examination subject. Experience in Malaysia has proven that transmitting values by using the examination approach has not as yet produced the desired results.

Change Agent

The challenge of this role is how to transform resistance to acceptance of change. People are reluctant to change unless they can be convinced of the benefits of change. There are many theories on change management. Most of them stress the need to explain clearly the purpose of change, the process involved and the expected beneficial results. Consideration must be given to certain cultural factors that inhibit change. To ensure success, often adjustment and modification of the original proposal have to be made to enhance the degree of acceptability.

One important aim of education when we move into the next millennium is to teach students how to cope with rapid and constant political, economic and social changes. Adaptability and flexibility are important skills.

Conflicts Mediator

Conflict or dissension is inherent in any organization, simple or complex. The Chinese hold the view that if there exist goodwill, sincerity, humility, willingness to see and appreciate different viewpoints, big conflicts can be reduced to small conflicts and small conflicts dissolved into no conflicts.

Once again, there are numerous theories on conflict management. A popular one is the WIN-WIN THEORY, very much used in the business world to settle disputes.

I refer you to a very interesting article I came across in the July, 1999 issue of *ALUMNUS*, a *NUS* publication (Chia and Chu 1999). The article entitled *Mediation Across Cultures* is by Dr. Chia and Mr. Chu. They discuss the different western and eastern approaches to mediating conflicts.

Finance Controller

As mentioned earlier, education is a capital intensive enterprise. It can be foreseen that increasing use of information technology will increase annual education budget by leaps and bounds. Although educators are not directly involved in managing finance, they are responsible for the proper implementation of financial procedures as laid down by the Ministry of Education and Ministry of Finance. A most careful supervision over disbursement of funds is essential to meet the requirements of accountability and transparency. It is stressed that it is not enough for a finance controller to be honest; he or she must be seen to be honest.

Evaluator

Evaluation must be a continuing process and shared effort. There are different types of evaluation, such as evaluating the performance of the entire school, evaluating different programmes of activities and evaluation of individual teacher's performance. Evaluation is a very demanding task that requires high level skills and specialised training. Computers are a blessing. Softwares are now available to meet the needs of different types of evaluation. They should be widely used to conserve energy and time. As mentioned under the role of management, evaluation is an integral part of the process of management.

Philosopher

Although listed last of the nine roles, it is the most important, over-riding all the other eight roles. *PHILOSOPHY IS THE FOUNDATION OF EDUCATION AND A JUST SOCIETY.*

Vision statements formulated by schools are essentially philosophical statements. All the problems and challenges that account for the complexity of education administration and the different roles of education administrators which have been analysed and discussed have philosophical implications. Philosophy is concerned with the WHY of education.

In an age when excessive importance is focussed on economic development and the development of science and technology, there is an urgent need to provide a balance with equal emphasis on culture and human values.

What society needs are not narrowly trained technocrats but educated technocrats who possess besides their own expertise, also wide interest in literature, music, drama, visual and the performing arts. It will be a sad world if technocrats and CEOs of the business world cannot communicate with people possessing different skills and interests.

Chinese philosophers are aware of the difficulties in producing an educated person. They formulated a saying:

It takes ten years to cultivate a tree, a hundred years to cultivate a person.
SHI NIAN SHU MU, BAI NIAN SHU REN.

The eight roles of education administrators represent the horizontal dimension with main emphasis on the professional development of teachers.

Hopefully, the brief comments on each of the nine roles of education administrators will convince practitioners that despite a centralised system of education, there is wide scope for creative management. It is in the professional aspect of education administration that education can exercise best their creative skills. In the past, this important area was often neglected.

Regional Centre for Education Administration

I would like to conclude my presentation with a proposal that Singapore will consider setting up a regional centre for education administration. There is a crying need for a centre totally committed to the study, teaching and research in education administration. Singapore possesses almost all the requirements that favour the setting up of an innovative regional centre.

1. There already exists in the National Institute of Education a very strong School of Policy and Management Studies.
2. There is a vast pool of very talented school principals.
3. The government can be relied upon to give the fullest support to a project that will enhance the quality of education.

4. Geographically, Singapore is ideally situated at the crossroad between continental and insular South East Asia and between India and China.
5. Singapore has excellent professional ties with countries in Asia and the Pacific Region, Europe and America through the channels of the Council of Education Administration and the South East Asia and the Pacific Region Administrators' and Managers' Symposium.

The curriculum will be learners centred, technology based and service oriented. A wide range of courses will be offered to cater to the needs of an equally wide range of education administrators.

The subjects must include not only those directly involved in the theory and practice of education administration but also Philosophy of Education, Sociology and Education, Comparative Education and other related disciplines to widen the perspective of education administrators.

In addition to a core of highly qualified staff with rich practical experience, local and foreign talents should be invited to participate in teaching and research.

Regularly school principals, school inspectors and senior teacher educators should be seconded to the centre to work as a team to teach and to develop programmes to cope with constant changes and new demands.

The centre will also serve as an informal meeting place to school principals, school inspectors, teacher educators, members of the school governing boards and those of parent-teacher associations and staff of the Ministry of Education to meet, interact and share experiences with one another.

Every effort must be made to break down barriers that isolate one group from another. Achieving excellence in education demands total commitment and happy partnership of all directly or indirectly involved in the administration and management of institutions of learning at all levels.

A strong regional centre will attract funding from outside Singapore and participation by foreign experts.

It can be envisaged that setting up a regional centre for education administration in Singapore will be a most exciting, challenging and rewarding venture. Both Dr. Ruth Wong in heaven and I look forward to its birth in the not too distant future.

Acknowledgements There are instances where we have been unable to trace or contact the copyright holder. If notified, the publisher will be pleased to rectify any errors or omissions.

Reference

Chia, H. B., & Chu, S. H. (1999, July). Mediation across cultures: Are we supplementing our cultural values through institutionalised mediation? *The AlumNUS*, *38*, 20–21.

Author Biography

Professor Chang started his career as Chief Inspector of Schools, West Malaysia. He then joined the Universiti Sains Malaysia, (USM) Pulau Pinang, Malaysia as Senior Lecturer in Education and Co-ordinator of the Off-campus Programme. From 1975 until his retirement in April 1978 he was Director for Centre of Educational Studies, USM. He is a well-known educator and author of many books and articles in education, particularly in teacher education in Malaysia. He was a Visiting Professor of Education at the University of Armidale, New South Wales, Australia.

Chapter 8
Education and Human Resources Development for the Knowledge Economy: A Personal Perspective

Hon Chan Chai

I want to ask three questions which might appear, at first glance, to have no obvious relation to one another. I hope, however, as I proceed the connections will become clear.

The three questions are, **first**, Why are some countries so much richer than so many others? **Second**, Who was Ruth Wong and what was her contribution to Singapore's educational development? And **third**, What did the World Bank do to help in the development of the National University of Singapore?

Why Are a Few Countries So Rich and the Majority So Poor?

Many countries have become much, much richer in monetary terms than they were even a decade ago. This is seen in the thousands, perhaps hundreds of thousands, of instant millionaires and billionaires who got rich through investments in the new companies that capitalized on the Internet. For example, a stock market analyst estimated that if someone had invested $10,000 in America Online (AOL) when it first offered shares to the public about 10 years ago, the market value of his AOL shares would be something like $10 million. True or not, this is a metaphor to illustrate how wealth—at least on paper—is growing in a country like the United States. So, by contrast, the poor countries appear to have become poorer. Poor countries lag behind the rich not because they have fewer natural resources but because they have less knowledge, and because their economy and their social and political environment are not conducive to the creation of knowledge. Lacking knowledge by itself, however, is not the root problem. The fundamental problem is

H.C. Chai (✉)
87 Jalan Cenderai 2, Lucky Garden Bangsar, 59100 Kuala Lumpur, Malaysia
e-mail: chai.honchan@gmail.com

© Springer Nature Singapore Pte Ltd. 2017
O.S. Tan et al. (eds.), *Global Voices in Education*,
DOI 10.1007/978-981-10-3539-5_8

the lack of knowledge on how to acquire, understand, adapt, use and recreate knowledge appropriate for specific purposes. The poor countries are poor because they lack the ability to use knowledge that has made the rich countries rich.

Most of the countries in East Asia started on the modernization road in the 1950s and 1960s as low-income economies. In about four decades, a few of these countries have closed, or nearly closed, the gap between them and the high income countries, while others continue to lag behind.

In 1999, the GDP per capita in US dollars was as follows for the countries in the region:[a]	
Singapore	28,518[b]
Hong Kong	22,738
Taiwan	13,095
South Korea	8691
Malaysia	3472
Thailand	1996
China	786
Indonesia	680
The figures for the developed countries in the region[a]	
Japan	38,117
Australia	20,442
New Zealand	13,862

[a]*Source* Goldman Sachs (1999)
[b]In 1967, Singapore's GDP per capita was US$592; in 1970, US$920; in 1991, US$14,500, second only to Japan's

What is the explanation for these enormous differences in GDP per capita among the countries? If we look to the classical theory of economic development, we won't find the answer. The old strategy for economic development was (a) to develop unused or poorly used land for more productive enterprises, agricultural or industrial; (b) to invest in physical infrastructure, such as ports, roads, telecommunications, factories; and (c) to expand education and training and increase the labour force.

It has been pointed that all the East Asian countries, according to their endowments, have done all these things. The amazing fact is that Singapore and Hong Kong, which have the highest and second highest per capita GDP, respectively, have virtually no land to speak of. Therefore, developing land did not significantly contribute to their economic growth. True, Singapore and Hong Kong invested strongly in physical infrastructure, but so did many of the other countries. They also put a lot of their resources into education and training. So did other countries. So, where is the difference?

The difference, the World Bank suggests, was that the richer East Asian countries were growing *smarter* as they built and worked hard on their way up the economic ladder. "Could knowledge, then," asks the World Bank, "have been behind East Asia's surge? If so, the implications are enormous, for that would mean that knowledge is the key to development—that knowledge *is* development." (World Bank 1998, p. 19).

The above statement, however, needs to be qualified. It seems an easy answer to a difficult question. It packs in many assumptions which should be teased out and carefully examined.

The truth is that there is no simple way to evaluate the effect of knowledge on economic growth. Emerging out of the debates in the 1950s, 1960s and 1970s on the causes of economic growth is a conclusion that is fairly well accepted: ***human capital*** has been a critical factor in generating and sustaining economic development.

Empirical studies have shown that higher levels of education resulted in more people being able to use technology more effectively. For example, farmers with primary education were far more productive through better understanding and use of fertilizer and crop rotation than those with no education. Technicians with secondary education work more efficiently with sophisticated machinery.

It is generally accepted that Hong Kong, South Korea, Singapore and Taiwan, the four fastest-growing East Asian economies, owe their success to their investment in education. Their strategy had the effect of closing the knowledge gap between the rich and the developing economies. The World Bank suggests that by investing in physical capital which embodied knowledge, and by investing in people and institutions to strengthen their capability to absorb and use knowledge, these four East Asian countries were able to bring themselves abreast of the rich countries. Indeed, in terns of GDP per capita, Hong Kong and Singapore have surpassed the per capita GDP of Australia and New Zealand. (Of course, we should keep in mind that higher per capita GDP is not the same thing as higher living standards, although the two are connected).

What other factors account for their economic success of the East Asian countries? The major factors included openness to innovation and receptiveness to new knowledge from abroad; the presence of supportive economic policies; the presence of strong, development-oriented institutions; and the presence of a dynamic and efficient public management system.

Into this powerful mix of preconditions, I would throw in **language facility**, specifically the ability to use an international language, such as English. Various studies show that employers of technically skilled staff require them to have communication skills—ability to understand and present technical reports, make oral presentations to visiting foreign business representatives, and so on. A functioning command of written English would be a major advantage for accessing the latest knowledge because practically all the latest information on research findings in technology, the physical and biological sciences, medicine, pharmaceuticals, and so on is available in English language publications. Is it a coincidence that Singapore, which has been rated as **the most competitive economy in the world** uses English as the main medium of teaching and learning in the education system from primary to tertiary level and as the language of public administration?

All the above factors, acting synergistically, are necessary conditions for the creation, acquisition, absorption, recreation, utilization and dissemination of knowledge.

Acquisition of Knowledge

How do developing countries go about widening and deepening their knowledge base? The most cost-effective way to grow their knowledge is to acquire technical and scientific know-how from developed countries which produce 80% of the world's research output through investment in research and development (R&D). Part of the economic success of the East Asian countries mentioned earlier is due to their importing and adapting tried and tested technology from the advanced countries.

There are several ways of acquiring knowledge from abroad. The **first** is through the imported goods and services that have become increasingly technology-intensive. **Second** is through foreign direct investment (FDI), which usually brings with it the latest technology. The quality of the technology, however, depends on the investment and trade policies of the receiving country. The more liberal policies that support an open-trade system will likely draw in competitive foreign investment with state-of-the-art technology and, equally important, the most effective management styles. Without effective management, the latest technology is unlikely to be used productively.

A **third** way is through licensing of foreign technology through which a developing country can access the latest and most competitive ideas on the production of goods and services. This would be much more cost effective than attempting to copy and adapt new technology through reverse engineering.

A **fourth** approach is the classic strategy of using public funds to send students to study abroad, bonding them to return to the home country when they graduate and bring back with them the latest in science and technology. Japan used this technique in the 19th century to modernize the country. When China opened its doors to modernization in the last quarter of the 20th century, it sent tens of thousands of students abroad, mostly to the United States, to learn the latest in science and technology and modern business management. The same pattern has been observed in Malaysia since the 1970s. This also must be true, to a lesser or greater degree, in other countries in East Asia.

However, the acquisition of the latest knowledge in science and technology is one thing. Its absorption and utilization is something else. The effective harnessing and productive use of new technology would depend on national policies, a supportive economic environment, and a far-sighted human resource development strategy and the productive use of human talent.

We have noted that Singapore and Hong Kong had the two highest per capita GDP in 1999 in the region. It is no coincidence that Singapore, with a long tradition of free trade, actively encouraged foreign investments as part of its development strategy. Over time and in step with changes in the world economy, the foreign investments shifted towards more complex technologies. A conducive environment was created by the government which built new facilities and rapidly expanded and modernized its industrial parks, seaport, airport, surface transportation system and telecommunications which, today, are among the best in East Asia.

At the same time, Singapore expanded and strengthened its education and training system to ensure a high quality work force to complement foreign investments (World Bank 1998). In the process of national development, the setting of ideals by leaders provides an important psychological reference point for the public. A high quality work force based on a high quality education system is the practical translation of Singapore's quest for excellence. The 1999 Global Competitiveness Report (Schwab et al. 1999), published by the Switzerland-based World Economic Forum, ranked Singapore, for the third year in a row, as the world's most competitive economy, ahead of Hong Kong which won second place; the United States, third place, and the United Kingdom, fourth place.

Similarly, Hong Kong, a bastion of free trade since its founding, followed a liberal development policy of low taxes and a stable environment for all investors, local and foreign, who made their own choice of whatever technology best suited to their enterprise. A modern rapid transit system and a new airport enhanced its already high quality physical infrastructure. At the same time, attention was given to improving the access to, and quality of education, particularly the secondary and tertiary sectors.

Absorption of Knowledge

In the 1950s and 1960s many developing countries thought that the shortage of capital was the main barrier to their economic growth. That was an incorrect perception. The truth was that they had a limited capacity to absorb capital, to put it to productive use. There are lots of stories about some developing countries getting expensive tractors but left them to rust in the sun and the rain when they broke down because they lacked technicians to maintain and repair them; or about costly science equipment left in their packing crates gathering dust because the teachers had not been trained to use them.

An analogous situation prevails today in many developing countries with regard to the absorption of knowledge. This is due to the fact that the exponential growth of knowledge has been so great that most education systems cannot catch up with it. So, like physical capital 30 or 40 years ago, knowledge and its absorption in the 21st century will depend on the availability of appropriately educated and trained people to monitor the utilization and further adaptation and dissemination of knowledge.

Clearly, the key lies in having a dynamic education and training system. A strong base must be laid in primary education, which provides the foundation for secondary and higher education, which will produce the management, technical and scientific workforce for a knowledge economy.

Countries approaching or are at the frontiers of science and technology would need to strengthen their higher education system and research institutions to keep their economies globally strong and competitive in knowledge absorption and creation. They must be positioned to teach better skills so that their graduates, working in various sectors of the economy, can monitor technological trends, adapt knowledge to national needs and help devise an effective technology strategy for the nation.

Higher education will need to not merely stay abreast of the knowledge revolution but be several steps ahead. There needs to be an appropriate mix of skills produced because the *type* of higher education has a strong bearing on economic growth. The proportion of science, mathematics and engineering graduates is positively associated with subsequent economic growth rates, suggesting that the *content* of higher education is very important.

The quality of higher education graduates depends on the quality of the primary and secondary education which made it possible for the graduates to enter tertiary education. And the key to the quality of education at all levels is clearly the teacher.

The quality of teachers—and they include principals, head teachers and supervisors who come from the ranks of teachers—is without doubt the main determinant of the quality of education, after taking into account all other factors, such as physical facilities, laboratories and workshops, textbooks and other instructional materials.

The topic of teachers brings me to one of the most distinguished personalities in Singapore's teaching profession.

Dr. Ruth Wong Hie King

Who was Dr. Ruth Wong Hie King? What did she achieve in education? What is her contribution to Singapore's educational development?

I remember Ruth Wong as a slim, gentle woman who looked taller than she really was because she carried no spare weight. Metaphorically, she always stood tall.

Her slender figure, however, belied a passionate and steely resolve to improve the practice of education so that the children who spend the most formative years of their life in the classroom would have the optimum learning experience. Her signature costume was always an elegantly tailored *cheongsam*. Her elegance and simplicity were set off by her jet-black hair neatly pulled back into a vertical roll at the back of her head. The only concession to ornament was a single strand of white pearls which she wore occasionally. Her horn-rimmed glasses gave her an air of confidence and authority, which might have conveyed the impression that she was cold and impersonal. In fact, she was warm-hearted, had a great sense of humour, and often shared jokes with her colleagues for a good laugh.

She was a dedicated educator who cared as much about people as she cared about ideas. She often counseled young people to be diligent and patient, reminding them they were building their future through their studies, citing her own experience of hard work in her youth. Her childhood experience of growing up as the eldest in the family helping to care for her younger siblings made her particularly empathetic with young people who were poor and deprived.

I know of two cases, one in Kuala Lumpur when Ruth Wong was Dean of the Education Faculty in the University of Malaya, and the other here in the National Institute of Education (NIE), in which she helped two young staff who, because of poverty had not completed secondary schooling. She personally tutored them in her spare time after office hours, to encourage them to take the examinations that would give them the secondary school qualifications so that they might have better prospects of employment. She also helped to pay their examination fees out of her own pocket.

Professionally, Dr. Ruth Wong laid the foundation for an analytical approach to teaching and learning, stressing the importance of linking practice to theory and strengthening theory with a continuous critical evaluation of what actually goes on in the classroom. She maintained that this was particularly important in the professional preparation of teachers, that the trainers of teachers are in touch with reality on the ground as well as with the latest thinking on all the disciplines that go into the menu of teacher education. She constantly reminded teachers that they should not lose sight of the central importance of their role—indeed, their mission—of facilitating the cognitive, emotive and social development of their students. In the few short years as its Director, Dr. Wong laid the institutional foundation of the National Institute of Education (NIE) whose strength, she rightly perceived, lay in developing the academic and professional competencies of faculty staff.

Details of Dr. Ruth Wong's life, her career and her achievements as an educator are very well documented in an excellent biography entitled, *The Educational Legacy of Dr. Ruth Wong Hie King* (Ho 1995) authored by Dr. Ho Wah Kam, a former Dean of the NIE. Suffice it for me to briefly sketch a profile.

Ruth Wong grew up as the eldest of ten children in a strongly-knit Christian family. Her father, who had settled in Singapore in 1916 from Fuzhou Province in China, was a highly respected lay preacher who also ran a tailoring business to support his family. From some family members, and a few former colleagues and students, we catch glimpses of her childhood. Even when she was very young, Ruth Wong was a caring sister to her siblings. She gave up a scholarship, when she successfully completed the Senior Cambridge examinations at the age of 16, to take up teaching in a private school for $26 a month to help support the family.

When she resumed her studies, Ruth Wong went from success to success. She graduated from Raffles College at the age of 20, winning an award for outstanding scholastic performance. After the Second World War, she studied at Queen's College, Belfast (1951–53) where she graduated with an honours degree in mathematics; and later at Harvard University (1962–63), where she graduated with a master's degree and a doctorate in education.

Returning to Singapore in 1963, Ruth Wong taught for a while at the School of Education in the University and the Teachers Training College, Singapore, before she moved to the University of Malaya in Kuala Lumpur to head the newly

established School of Education, later the Faculty of Education where she became
the first Dean and Professor of Education.

The six years she spent in Kuala Lumpur as the first woman Professor of
Education and Dean of the Faculty helped establish her reputation as an educator.
They also gave her a valuable insight into the complexities of education in multiethnic societies where national educational policies have to balance and moderate
competing and often conflicting communal interests. Along with nurturing the
development of the new Faculty of Education, Ruth Wong tried to introduce
innovative approaches to teaching and learning by instituting a laboratory school
affiliated with the Faculty to link theory with actual educational practice. But the
social and political conditions that prevailed after 1965, when Singapore left the
federation of Malaysia, were not conducive to the kind of experimental studies in
education that she considered important in developing a local source of knowledge.
Ruth Wong felt that, as a Singaporean, she should return to serve the infant
Republic, which had been established in August 1965 after Singapore ceased to be
part of Malaysia. In 1969 Ruth Wong returned to Singapore as the Director of
Research in the Ministry of Education and simultaneously (from mid-1971)
Principal of the Teachers Training College (TTC) which became the sole teacher
training institution for primary and secondary school teachers when the School of
Education in the University of Singapore was closed at the end of 1971. In April
1973, the TTC itself was replaced by the Institute of Education, with Ruth Wong as
its first Director. The academic and professional programmes for teacher education
were revamped in response to the changing needs of education in Singapore.

At the same time, Dr. Wong re-defined the Institute's relationship with the school
system by setting up a School of Continuing Studies which would offer courses for
teachers and educators who needed to keep abreast of the continuing increase in
knowledge. Dr. Wong envisaged a teaching career as lifelong learning. Addressing
the Teachers' Christian Fellowship, Ruth Wong said the teacher "will find a lifetime
of intellectual stimulation. However routine the school round, each day brings new
questions and new insights. The teacher is a perpetual learner.... There is much to
read about: new subjects, updated methods and approaches to teaching, the needs of
children, behavior modification and change, and so on.... Teaching has a rejuve-
nating effect on the teacher for it is association with the young that keeps him young
in outlook, while accruing wisdom through the years" (Ho 1995, p. 22).

Dr. Wong took the lead in reviewing and restructuring the teacher training
curriculum as part of a strategy to position teacher training in the vanguard of
Singapore's education and human resource development. She appealed for a
cross-disciplinary approach, emphasising the use of objectives, staff cooperation
and the introduction of research-based projects and assignments to replace some
examination papers (Ho 1995).

The new teacher education curriculum emphasized several interlocking processes: linking theory and practice in developing teachers' classroom skills; fostering their personal professional development; strengthening student teachers'
ability to think critically and creatively; and raising their awareness of national and
international issues. Clearly, the aim was to integrate the development of teaching

skills, nurturing personal inquiry and sharpening awareness of local and international problems (Ho 1995).

Ruth Wong frequently stressed the importance of strengthening the teacher-student relationship as part of the process of nurturing children. In a paper presented at the Guidance for Youth convention in 1975, she reminded the gathering that "it should always be remembered that the pupils we teach are possessed of soul, spirit, body as well as mind. It is not enough to rest our judgment on mere scholastic attainment. Feelings, attitudes, values, health characteristics besides mental ability enter into the making of the whole person" (Ho 1995, p. 20).

Nurturing children, adolescents or adults is, in a broad sense, nurturing creativity. In 1971, addressing the Singapore National Academy of Sciences, Ruth Wong declared, "Above all, creativity must be encouraged and fostered for, ironically, with highly successful industrialization, man creates obsolescence. If at any time, there is the need for innovation, this is the age. Innovation derives from creativity; there is no such thing as a purely intuitive hunch in the creative act. Underlying it there has to be persistence with ideas. Ideas come with thought, and thought by a difficult process of application whereby education and experience are brought to bear on diverse observations" (Ho 1995, p. 16). These words although expressed a generation ago, apply with equal force today.

From her experience as Dean and Professor of Education in the Faculty of Education, in Kuala Lumpur, Ruth Wong realized that an institution derived its strength and reputation primarily from the quality of the teaching staff. From the outset, therefore, she got the pledge of the University and the Ford Foundation to support an extensive staff development programme. This enabled her to secure for young academic staff leave to study for the doctoral degree overseas, the majority of staff going to Harvard and Stanford.

When Dr. Wong assumed the post of Principal of the Singapore TTC, she was the only person with a doctoral degree in education. Even when the NIE was founded, the number of doctoral degree staff could be counted on the fingers of one hand. Dr. Wong started a staff development programme supported by a government grant of S$1 million, which was a large sum of money in the early 1970s. It was an expensive investment in teacher education whose returns could not be assured even in the long run. The subsequent growth and development of NIE fully justified Dr. Wong's commitment to staff development as part of her vision of NIE's overall, long-term institutional development. By 1980, NIE had reached a level of staff quality that an external assessor declared would compare favourably with standards in Australia, New Zealand and the United Kingdom.

Today, NIE stands out as one of the premier teacher education institutions in East Asia. Its graduates are among the best educated and professionally prepared teachers in the region. The fact that the United Kingdom has sought to recruit teachers from Singapore is perhaps the most eloquent testimonial to the professional excellence of NIE. Ruth Wong would have laughed with delight at the sweet irony of witnessing Britain, the former colonial master, entrusting the education of British children to the teachers from a former colony. With such a wonderful tribute, it would be difficult to challenge the claim that Singapore's current level of socio-economic development is due to the quality of education, which in turn is due to the quality of teachers. In the final accounting, the quality of teachers will be a key determinant of Singapore's continuing success in the knowledge-based economy.

Education and Human Resource Development: The World Bank's Contribution

In recent years, the World Bank, together with its sister organization, the International Monetary Fund, has received a lot of bad press from many quarters. Among other things, the Bank has been charged with failing to help the poor countries. These charges stem partly from the fact that a significant proportion of the Bank's investment projects in education did not achieve their objectives, or were not sustainable even when implementation was successfully completed. But the criticisms arise also out of ignorance of what Bank-assisted education projects actually aimed to achieve compared with what actually happened on the ground[1] and the reasons for what happened.

For the last four decades, the Bank has been in the business of helping developing countries strengthen, improve and broaden their education and training systems to increase the number of skilled people to help grow the economy and improve the lives of the people. Bank investment projects in education covered primary, secondary and higher education; vocational, technical and agricultural education; teacher training and often special programmes called project-related training in conjunction with projects dealing with agriculture and infrastructure projects which required specialized technical or management training.

While many projects have a large physical construction and equipment procurement component, which may account for 70–80% of total project costs, the Bank's emphasis is on the 'software' aspects, the educational objectives, such as improving access to schooling; raising the quality and efficiency of education and improving equity where a significant proportion of girls or ethnic minorities is not enrolled. Increasingly, greater attention is given to strengthening the planning and

---

[1]The World Bank is a development institution that provides loans and credits to borrowers to finance development projects in all key sectors of the economy, such as agriculture, transportation, health and education. Generally, low-income countries are eligible for credits which carry a nominal interest charge and are repaid over a longer period, while higher-income countries are eligible for loans which carry near-market interest rates and are repaid over a shorter period. All loans and credits are made to the government.

management capabilities of the borrowing countries to ensure the sustainability of the investments.

Project failure or success is related to a number of factors: the project design, the quality of project management, the economic and policy environment, the availability of post-implementation government funding to follow up on project initiated activities, and macroeconomic effects on labour markets which may affect the employment of graduates in the case of secondary or higher education projects.

A well-designed project is a prerequisite for successful implementation and operation. Designing a World Bank project is time-consuming because the Bank must ensure that all relevant information is available for making an informed judgment on the viability of the project. The Bank has to ensure that project inputs, such as buildings, equipment and staff training, are directly related to its objectives, and that the appropriate output or impact indicators are established for monitoring and evaluating achievement of the objectives. For the borrowing countries, the process of designing and implementing a project provides the key lessons that could help to strengthen their planning and management system.

Two examples of the Bank's contribution to institutional development in China and Singapore should show how benefits flow from investment projects in education.

In 1999, China successfully completed a teacher education project which assisted 124 teacher training institutions with a combined total enrolment of 205,000 spread over 15 provinces which had a total population of about 763 million people. With a total investment of US$256 million, the project was designed to improve the quality of teacher training and the planning and management of teacher training, and to facilitate innovation in teacher training and classroom teaching.

Although the hardware and software inputs (buildings and equipment; staff training, teaching/learning materials, library books, and so on) were important, it was the innovation programme that was the most challenging, with the most significant impact on modernising the teacher training system. With only a US$5 million budget, about 2% of the total project, the project provided a powerful stimulus to quality improvement through innovation programmes based on 460 action-research sub-projects on teaching science, mathematics and English. They were organized and monitored by a team comprising national academicians and key Ministry of Education officials.

The scale and quality of the research sub-projects were unprecedented in the history of teacher education in China. They unleashed the research potential and enhanced the quality of teaching in the teacher training institutions. All this was made possible by dedicated and effective leadership and the intellectual readiness of teaching staff to find ways to improve on the traditional ways of teaching. The success was due to institutional support and a critical mass of adequately trained manpower to absorb, improve, recreate, apply and disseminate new ideas and methods on teaching and learning. The innovations are expected to be disseminated through the 124 teacher training institutions and beyond them to the rest of the country. The long-term impact is expected to be on the quality of secondary education. The improved quality is then expected to feed into higher education.

In Singapore, the World Bank helped finance the re-development, in two phases, of the former University of Singapore at the new Kent Ridge campus.[2] The overall objective was to improve the quality of university graduates through better teaching and research facilities to help meet the estimated future demand for high level manpower.

The two phases, completed in 1978 and 1981, respectively, were among the most successful education development projects funded by the World Bank. They assisted in the consolidation at the Kent Ridge campus of the Faculties of Engineering and Architecture and the School of Accountancy and Business Administration, and the development of the Faculties of Science, Arts and Social Sciences and Law, the Central Library, and the various administrative and communal facilities.

The speedy and efficient *implementation* of the two phases was attribute to the University of Singapore Development Unit (USDU), headed by an experienced architect and a team of architects, engineers, accountants, and other specialist staff. The active participation of academic staff in project implementation also contributed to project success.

Would the National University of Singapore have achieved its present status as a world class higher education institution without the assistance of the World Bank? It is an intriguing 'What might have been' question to which there is no straight answer. If the question is set in the historical context, some answers would suggest themselves.

Recall that Singapore's destiny was at the crossroads in 1967/68 when the World Bank was approached for assistance in developing the young Republic's higher education system. With a per capita GDP of US$592 in 1967, Singapore was a Third World country with no natural resources, no viable domestic market and, most worrisome of all, set in what was then perceived as an unfriendly, not to say hostile, environment. The timing could not have been worse for Great Britain's announcement that she would phase out, by 1971, its Singapore military bases. The British military bases contributed an estimated US$150 million equivalent or 13% of Singapore's GDP. Singapore faced the spectre of rising unemployment.

With hardly any silver lining in the dark clouds overshadowing the island, Singapore needed the reassurance of an international organization, such as the World Bank, to support the plan to invest in a key human resource sector that would

---

[2]The combined estimated cost of Phase I (started 1971, completed 1978) and Phase II (started 1974, completed 1981) was US$62 million, of which US$29 million was financed by two Bank loans and the rest financed by the government.

determine the economic, if not the political, future of the Republic. Getting a loan from the World Bank was not the main point. After all, the loan for Phase I was only US$9.5 million, a relatively modest sum that Singapore could have raised itself without much difficulty. By 1980, Singapore was declared by the Bank that the Republic was rich enough to raise development funds on its own.

Whatever the reasons for Singapore's initial borrowing, the World Bank's involvement fulfilled the government's objective of helping in the university's development of high level, high quality technological manpower to take Singapore's industrialization to a higher level.

Whatever conclusion one may draw from the historical background, the point is that the World Bank serves as a facilitator, a catalyst to development which, ultimately, is the result of the determination and hard work of the leaders and the technocrats and administrators in the country concerned.

The National University of Singapore has come a long way since its move to Kent Ridge. Its evolution into a world class institution of higher learning is due to, among other things, sound planning and administration, an enlightened policy of maintaining a mix of local and expatriate academic staff, provision of top rate facilities for teaching, study, research and student residence and recreation. It has one of the best libraries in the region.

> NUS is moving in the right direction", declared the new Vice-Chancellor, Professor Shih Choon Fong. With bright, young students, resourceful staff and talented faculty members committed to teaching and research, NUS should prepare students not only for careers in Singapore but should nurture them to be "citizens of the world, versatile and alert to global as well as local opportunities... (Shih 2000, p. 4).

Professor Shih shares the view that education is the soundest investment a nation can make. "Knowledge and talent are central resources in the new economy", he says, "and education is the key to developing knowledge and talent. It is imperative for knowledge in the new economy to be dynamic, comprising three interdependent processes of creating, imparting and applying" (Shih 2000, p. 5).

Believing that knowledge can be constantly created, invalidated, destroyed and then recreated, Professor Shih advises that Singapore should recruit "the best" to be teachers "because teachers create that multiplying effect. They also inspire our students to fulfill their dreams of becoming professionals, entrepreneurs, scholars and leaders of society" (Shih 2000, p. 5).

I can imagine Dr. Ruth Wong applauding.

And so we come full circle to the argument that it is not knowledge or external capital, **per se**, that helps, let alone determines, the direction and scope of a country's economic and social development. It is the capacity to absorb, harness, adapt, recreate, utilize and disseminate knowledge that is crucial to a country's successful transformation from a traditional economy to a knowledge economy. That capacity can be achieved only when the education system provides opportunities at all levels for life-long learning, and the quality of the education system is determined by the quality of its teachers.

References

Ho, W. K. (1995). *The educational legacy of Dr. Ruth Wong Hie King*. Singapore: Centre for Applied Research in Education.

Shih, C. F. (2000, July). NUS new Vice-Chancellor, *The AlumNUS, July 2000*(42), 4–5.

World Bank. (1998). *World Development Report 1998/1999: Knowledge for development*. New York, NY: Oxford University Press.

Schwab, K., Porter, M. E., Sachs, J. D., Warner, A. M., & Levinson, M. (Eds.). (1999). *The global competitiveness report 1999*. New York, NY: Oxford University Press.

Author Biography

Professor Hon-Chan Chai, Ed.D (Harvard, USA), M.A., B.A. Hons (Adelaide, Australia) was Professor of Education at the University of Malaya from 1971 to 1981 and Dean, Faculty of Education (1971–1974). He started his career as a teacher and taught primary and secondary classes in English Language and literature, religious knowledge, Latin and Biology. As lecturer and later Professor of Education he was responsible for courses in Comparative Education, methodology of history teaching and human resource development. Whilst in Guyana as a visiting lecturer he did a field research and at the request of the World Bank prepared an education-manpower development plan for the Ministry of Education Guyana (1967). His interests include second language acquisition and its implications for education and human resource development in developing countries. In 1978 whilst still with the University of Malaya he acted as Project Officer for the World Bank in the development of the Singapore University at Kent Ridge. After leaving the University of Malaya in 1981 he continued with the World Bank as education specialist and consultant responsible for the implementation and supervision and later for the appraisal and evaluation of primary, secondary and higher education investment projects in Bangladesh, Indonesia, Philippines, Thailand, Solomon Islands & Vanuata. After his formal retirement from the World Bank in 1995, he remained as consultant on Bank education investment projects in Bangladesh, China, Malaysia, Philippines and Thailand. His many publications include *Planning education for a plural society* (Paris: Unesco, ILEP, 1971); *Education and nation-building in plural societies: The West Malaysian experience* (Canberra: Australian National University, Development Studies Centre, 1977); *The sustainability of investment projects in education 1990*, (with David Throsby, School of Economic and Financial Studies, Macquarie University, Australia); *Policy, planning and management of distance education for teacher education* (with Hena Mukherjee) in *Teacher education through open and distance learning* (London: Routledge and Falmer, 2003).

Chapter 9
Women and Leadership in Institutions of Higher Education

Jasbir Kaur

Introduction

> Whereas the hope is that "academic life...is a sphere where in theory, women should find few barriers to opportunity" the reality seems to be that "academia ...has been perceived as traditionally elitist, male and patriarchal in its workplace culture, structure and values" (Lund 1998, p. 1).

Over the last three decades, both in industrialised and newly industrialising countries, women have taken great strides to improve their participation in higher education: girls' attendance at all levels of education has improved and in many countries more girls attend school than boys; more women are in undergraduate programmes often in numbers comparable to men; and more women also enroll in postgraduate studies, and take up employment in higher education institutions. In the U.S.A. and Canada, western Europe, Australia and New Zealand, as well as in Hong Kong, Malaysia, Singapore, and Thailand, women today easily make up 50% of all undergraduate enrolments (although they concentrate in traditional female areas), and they generally constitute half of all academic and most of support (clerical) staff.

J. Kaur (✉)
10-01 Block B, Cameron Towers, Jalan 5/58B, 46000 Petaling Jaya, Selangor, Malaysia
e-mail: jasbirkd37@gmail.com

Consultant to the Association of Commonwealth Universities' Gender Programme, London, UK

Former Professor of Sociological Studies, Faculty of Education, University of Malaya, Kuala Lumpur, Malaysia

Former Chief Programme Officer (Higher Education Co-operation), Commonwealth Secretariat, London, UK

© Springer Nature Singapore Pte Ltd. 2017
O.S. Tan et al. (eds.), *Global Voices in Education*,
DOI 10.1007/978-981-10-3539-5_9

While universities pride themselves on achievement of such numerical 'equity', inequality prevails in their occupational levels and promotional opportunities (Luke 1999). In all countries, almost without exception, women occupy the lower levels of the institutions; their numbers decrease significantly in the upper echelons of academia. Data from many countries have made it apparent that the domain of administrative leaderships in higher education remains the domain of men.

A 1993 UNESCO-Commonwealth report on women in higher education management showed that "with hardly an exception the global picture is one of men outnumbering women at about five to one at middle management level and at about twenty to one at senior management level.... Women deans and professors are a minority group and women vice-chancellors and presidents are still a rarity" (Dines 1993, p. 11). An Association of Commonwealth Universities (ACU) survey showed that by 2000, the situation had improved only marginally. At middle management level men outnumber women at about 3 or 4 to one and at senior management level men outnumber women at about ten to one. Women vice-chancellors/presidents, deans and professors are still a minority, 9.0, 14.3 and 13.1% respectively (Singh 2002a).

However, in most countries, a small proportion of women are beginning to reach the top management positions in higher education institutions as vice-chancellors, deputy vice-chancellors, deans and heads of departments. They now provide role models for those beginning their careers in higher education.

The subject of women in higher education has received considerable attention in recent years. The status of women has been well monitored, considerable research has been undertaken to identify factors that work against women's advancement in the higher education sector. Many countries have legislated and put affirmative action in place to assist academic women advance. Many international agencies such as UNESCO and the Commonwealth Secretariat have also adopted programmes that target women's development. Associations of universities such as ACU and individual universities have established their own women in leadership programmes and projects.

As a result of all this activity, we are today much better informed about the status of women and we have considerable knowledge about what causes women to improve their career prospects. We have a great deal of instructive material from all the affirmative action and women in leadership programmes, to help us plan strategies and plans of action to alleviate the status of women in higher education institutions.

In view of the above, this lecture will attempt to provide you with an overview, based largely on Commonwealth materials, of the current status of women in higher education, with a focus on the Asian countries, with some comparison with countries that have had greater success in promoting women into management positions; identify factors disabling women; note some of the real inequities women experience; suggest strategies to improve the status of women in higher education management; and point to some success in improving women's status through the institution of special women in leadership programmes.

Gender Distribution in Universities

Overall Gender Distribution

The ACU published a report on female numbers in Commonwealth Universities, *A Single Sex Profession?* (Lund 1998). This was followed by an update, *Still a Single Sex Profession?* (Singh 2002b). With data in 2000 limited to academic staff above the level of senior lecturer, the survey revealed that women were severely under-represented at all upper levels of the academic and administrative hierarchies of Commonwealth universities.

At the senior lecturer and above level, in 2000, there were 28,310 women from a total of 125,212, representing 22.6% of all academic staff employed in universities at this level.

On the whole, at this level of employment, no discernible difference was evident between universities in developing and developed countries of the Commonwealth. All the developed countries had between 22 and 24% women working at senior lecturer and above level (Table 9.1).

Among countries employing the highest proportion of women at senior levels were a number of developing countries: Guyana (33.0%), Jamaica (39.6%), Sri Lanka (31.5%) and Swaziland (29.2%). A number of developing countries had around 20% women employed at this level in universities: Brunei Darussalam, Fiji, Hong Kong, India, Lesotho, Malaysia, Mauritius, Pakistan, Sierra Leone, and South Africa. Among countries with the lowest percentage of women at senior levels were mostly developing countries: Cyprus, Kenya, Malta, Papua New Guinea.

Senior Women Managers, 2000

The findings of the survey are summarised in Table 9.2.

Top management positions continue to be the domain of men. As chief executives, women were poorly represented. In 2000, there were only 9.0% women vice-chancellors and presidents in the Commonwealth. At this level, Asian countries performed very poorly. Pakistan, Bangladesh, Malaysia and Singapore had no woman chief executive, while India had only 7.2% women vice-chancellors, many of them in women's universities and Sri Lanka had one women vice-chancellor of the 11 vice-chancellors or 9.1%. The developed countries seemed to perform slightly better. Australia had appointed 8 (18.6%) women vice-chancellors from its 43 vice-chancellors, Canada had appointed 16 (18.4%) women presidents of its 87 presidents, and the United Kingdom had 12 (8.9%) women vice-chancellors of its 135 vice-chancellors/rectors.

Women heads of administration too remained a minority. Across the Commonwealth universities, only 14.9% heads of administration were women. In the Asian countries women were very poorly represented in these positions:

Table 9.1 Overall gender proportions by Country

Country	Women	As %	Men	As %	Total
Australia	3787	23.9	12,081	76.1	15,868
Bangladesh	427	13.0	2846	87.0	3273
Botswana	44	18.0	201	82.0	245
Brunei Darussalam	29	20.6	112	79.4	141
Cameroon	30	13.8	187	86.2	217
Canada	5618	22.6	19,196	77.4	24,814
Cyprus	7	9.2	69	90.8	76
Fiji	33	23.2	109	76.8	142
Ghana	96	12.3	683	87.7	779
Guyana	29	33.0	59	67.0	88
Hong Kong	245	19.2	1034	80.8	1279
India	3067	23.2	10,155	76.8	13,222
Jamaica	126	39.6	192	60.4	318
Kenya	146	12.4	1031	87.6	1177
Lesotho	20	21.1	75	78.9	95
Malawi	29	14.1	177	85.9	206
Malaysia	528	24.8	1603	75.2	2131
Malta	34	12.4	241	87.6	275
Mauritius	22	22.2	77	77.8	99
Mozambique	7	17.1	34	82.9	41
Namibia	26	52.0	24	48.0	50
New Zealand	702	22.7	2397	77.3	3099
Nigeria	703	15.1	3957	84.9	4660
Pakistan	467	22.9	1571	77.1	2038
Papua New Guinea	22	10.8	182	89.2	204
Sierra Leone	15	22.1	53	77.9	68
Singapore	367	17.2	1766	82.8	2133
South Africa	1287	23.9	4102	76.1	5389
Sri Lanka	496	31.5	1078	68.5	1574
Swaziland	28	29.2	68	70.8	96
Tanzania	61	14.2	368	85.8	429
Uganda	62	17.8	287	82.2	349
United Kingdom	9701	24.0	30,696	76.0	40,397
Zambia	25	14.3	150	85.7	175
Zimbabwe	24	36.9	41	63.1	65
Commonwealth	28,310	22.6	96,902	77.4	125,212

Bangladesh and Pakistan had no women heads of administration while Malaysia had 16.7% (1 of 6 reported), Singapore 50% (1 of 2) and Sri Lanka 9.1% (1 of 11). In the appointment of women as heads of administration, the developed

Table 9.2 Percentage senior women managers in Asia

	CEOs	Admin Heads	Finance Officers	SMT	Deans
Bangladesh %	0.0	0.0	0.0	10.3	4.2
N	0/15	0/13	0/11	3/29	2/48
India %	7.2	4.5	2.9	12.0	20.7
N	10/138	6/132	2/67	23/192	78/376
Malaysia %	0.0	16.7	0.0	15.6	16.4
N	0/9	1/6	0/4	5/32	12/73
Pakistan %	0.0	0.0	0.0	13.2	14.6
N	0/33	0/29	0/15	5.38	7/48
Singapore %	0.0	50.0	100.0	26.7	5.6
N	0/2	½	3/3	4/15	1/18
Sri Lanka %	9.1	9.1	30.0	38.5	18.0
N	1/11	1/11	3/10	10/26	9/50
Commonwealth	9.0	14.9	12.0	19.8	14.3
	54/602	79/531	45/374	329/1335	308/2160

Commonwealth countries had made greater progress. In Australia 20% (8 of 40), in Canada 34.3% (24 of 70), in New Zealand 12.5% (1 of 8), and in the United Kingdom, 23.2% (26 of 112) registrars/secretaries were women.

The position of finance officer was very largely occupied by men with only 12.0% finance officers across the Commonwealth being women. Among the Asian countries only Singapore and Sri Lanka had appointed women as finance officers: in Singapore all three finance officers were women and in Sri Lanka 3 of the 10 finance officers were women. The situation was not very different in the developed Commonwealth countries. In Australia 12.2% (5 of 41), in Canada 20.0% (9 of 45) and in the United Kingdom 14.1% (14 of 99) finance officers were women. In New Zealand, however, all such positions were taken up by men.

Of the senior management team (SMT), comprising deputy vice-chancellors, deputy presidents, registrars, special advisers, only 19.8% were women. Among the Asian countries, Singapore and Sri Lanka had appointed a significant number of women to the SMT, 26.7 and 38.5% respectively. Appointments in Bangladesh, Malaysia, Pakistan and India ranged between 10 and 15% of the SMT, below the Commonwealth average. There were greater numbers of women in the developed Commonwealth countries engaged in senior management. However, except in the case of Canada, they represented around 20% of the total positions in these countries. In Canada 32.1% (76 of 237) of these positions were held by women, but in Australia 20.0% (42 of 210), in New Zealand 20.8% (5 of 24) and in the United Kingdom 18.6% (98 of 528) were part of the senior management team in universities.

Deanships also continued to be held largely by men. There were only 14.3% women deans in the Commonwealth. India (20.7%), Sri Lanka (18.0%), Malaysia (16.4%) had made some progress in this domain. Appointments in Bangladesh and Singapore were regrettably low, 4.2% or 2 of 48 and 5.6% or 1 of 18 respectively.

The developed Commonwealth countries had about 10–20% women deans; among these Canada had the highest proportion of women deans, 19.0% or 55 of 290 deans.

Women in Senior Academic Positions

In academic leadership positions women have shown greater advancement than in administrative positions. Appointment of women as heads of academic departments and directors of academic centres was somewhat more encouraging than the appointment of deans. Overall Commonwealth proportion of women heads of departments was 17.9% and every country reported at least one woman head of department. All the Asian countries except Bangladesh (6.4%) and Singapore (13.9) had appointed women heads in proportions higher than the Commonwealth average. Surprisingly, in three of the four developed Commonwealth countries the proportion of women heads/directors hovered just above 15%—Australia (18.6% or 428 of 2304), New Zealand (15.8% or 58 of 367) and the United Kingdom (16.1% or 609 of 3775). Canada alone in this group reported more than 20% (21.3% or 419 of 1968) women heads/directors.

Overall in the Commonwealth, 13.1% of professors were women. Women in India, Malaysia, Pakistan and Sri Lanka had done fairly well at this level with 18.0, 16.9, 23.0 and 21.5% respectively. Only in Bangladesh (9.8%) and Singapore (6.6%) were there fewer women professors than the Commonwealth norm. Singapore had the lowest proportion of women professors among the Asian countries surveyed. The developed countries—Australia, Canada, New Zealand and the United Kingdom, had appointed between 10 and 20% women professors (Table 9.3).

Table 9.3 Percentage women in senior academic positions

	Professors	Assoc. Professors	Dept Heads	Chief Librarians
Bangladesh	9.8 129/1322	n.a	6.4 15/234	22.2 2/9
India	18.0 769/4273	30.8 1354/4397	21.6 433/2003	23.2 13/56
Malaysia	16.9 77/456	n.a	22.3 65/292	85.7 6/7
Pakistan	23.0 78/339	n.a	22.0 53/241	38.5 5/13
Singapore	6.6 11/167	19.5 34/174	13.9 20/144	0.0 0/1
Sri Lanka	21.5 29/135	34.9 336/964	25.3 74/293	60.0 6/10
Commonwealth	13.1 4349/33241	27.0 10779/39907	17.9 2686/15017	37.2 126/339

Again for the position of associate professor, Asian women have done well, better than most of their Commonwealth colleagues. In India and Sri Lanka especially the proportion of women associate professors is encouraging, 30.8 and 34.9% respectively. Overall, in the Commonwealth there were 27.0% women working as associate professors, readers, principal lecturers and senior lecturers. While this was a much higher proportion than women professors, even at this academic level, men outnumbered women by almost four to one. We can conclude that women were still not waiting in large numbers in the wings to step up to more senior management or academic positions. They were still working largely as lecturers or as part-time workers.

Women have done much better in taking up positions of chief librarian. Throughout the Commonwealth countries in the survey, 37.2% of the chief librarians were women. In Bangladesh and India women were still not in a dominant position in this job but in Malaysia and Sri Lanka there were more women chief librarians than men. In the developed Commonwealth countries women comprised nearly 50% of chief librarians. In Australia, 48.5% (16 of 33), in Canada, 54.8% (23 of 42) and in New Zealand, 50.0% chief librarians were women. Only in the United Kingdom women had not made such strides into this position, with only 28.3% (26 of 92) women chief librarians in their universities.

Women in Second Tier Management Positions

In addition to staff in very senior management positions, data were also obtained for a selected number of senior university staff with special administrative duties. These included those with responsibilities for personnel, computing services, development and/or fund raising, staff development and training, public relations, international offices, equal opportunity or equity offices, quality assurance and accreditation, and strategic planning.

The survey revealed that while women were well represented in these jobs, on the whole, they did not take up even 50% of jobs in Commonwealth universities. Moreover, women were likely to be concentrated in a few jobs seen as more suitable for women officers. Women were in fairly good numbers in staff development and equity offices, and moderately present as leaders in personnel, public relations, international offices and quality assurance. However, senior positions in computing, development and strategic planning were clearly seen as men's jobs. The average for the Commonwealth was 32.6% of personnel officers, 13.1% computing officers, 28.2% development officers, 42.5% staff development officers, 39.4% public relations officers, 32.9% international officers, 65.3% equity officers, 32.3% quality.

In Singapore, personnel matters were very much in the hands of women, both personnel officers reported were women while Malaysia had one of its four personnel officers women. And in Sri Lanka 4 of the 13 personnel officers were women. Bangladesh and Pakistan had no women personnel officers while India had only 2 of the 27 personnel officers or 7.4% women personnel officers. In the developed Commonwealth countries women had made greater strides to take up personnel jobs. In all four countries more than 35% personnel officers were women: in Australia, 35% (14 of 40), in Canada, 41.5% (17 of 41), in New Zealand, 40.0% (2 of 5) and in the United Kingdom, 38.9% (37 of 95) personnel officers were women.

Even in the case of appointing staff development officers, among Asian countries, only Singapore and Malaysia had appointed a significant proportion of women, 66.7 and 50% respectively. All the Indian subcontinent countries had appointed less than 20% women staff into these positions. Again, as in the case of many of the administrative positions within universities, women in the developed Commonwealth countries had made greater advances into the field of staff development/training than women in the developing Commonwealth countries. In Australia 58.3% (21 of 36), in Canada 48.5% (16 of 33), in New Zealand 42.9% (3 of 7) and in the United Kingdom 57.5% (50 of 87) staff development/training posts were with women (Table 9.4).

In public relations too, Singapore and Malaysia had appointed more women than other developing Commonwealth countries, but their numbers were few. Of the six public relations officers reported from Bangladesh none was a woman, and from Pakistan only one of eight was a woman. It was in the developed countries of the Commonwealth that women had participated actively in public relations work in universities. In Australia, 37.5% or 12 of 32 public relations jobs were in the hands of women. In Canada and the United Kingdom, more than 50% employed in public relations were women: 53.3% (16 of 30) in Canada and 55.9% (33 of 59) in the United Kingdom. However, in New Zealand only 25% (1 of 4) public relations officers were women.

Similarly, in the appointment of international officers, more women were appointed in Malaysia, Singapore and Sri Lanka, 3 of 6, 1 of 2, and 2 of 3 respectively, than in Bangladesh, India or Pakistan. In the developed Commonwealth countries, the post of international officer was well established in nearly all the universities. Women had made considerable inroads into this field of employment, taking up nearly 32–49% of the available positions. In Australia, 31.6% (12 of 38) international officers were women. Canada had the highest number of women international officers, 48.7% (19 of 39). In New Zealand, women comprised 40% (2 of 5) and in the United Kingdom, women made up 36.1% (30 of 83) of international officers.

The developed Commonwealth countries showed greater sensitivity to equal opportunity issues pertaining to gender, ethnicity and disabled groups. Nearly every university had made an appointment to head a unit or centre to develop and to ensure the implementation of equitable policies and practices. In four of the developed Commonwealth countries women dominated this area of employment. In Australia, 87.9% (29 of 33) equal opportunity officers were women. In Canada, women comprised 70.6% (12 of 17), in New Zealand, 66.7% (4 of 6) and in the United Kingdom, 72.1% (44 of 61) equal opportunity officers.

In the areas of strategic planning and computing and finance etc., even in developed Commonwealth countries the majority of appointees were men.

Table 9.4 Percentage women in second tier management positions

	Personnel Officers	Computing	Development	Staff Development	Public Relations	International Office	Equity	Quality Assurance	Strategic Planning
Bangladesh	0.0 0/5	0.0 0/7	0.0 0/7	20.0 1/5	0.0 0/6	0.0 0/3	100.0 1/1	0.0 0/1	0.0 0/0
India	7.4 2/27	9.5 4/42	5.0 2/40	6.9 2/29	10.0 2/20	0.0 0/20	0.0 0/1	0.0 0/13	0.0 0/2
Malaysia	25.0 1/4	0.0 0/5	25.0 1/4	66.7 2/3	25.0 1/4	50.0 3/6	0.0 0/0	0.0 0/0	0.0 0/0
Pakistan	0.0 0/9	0.0 0/9	0.0 0/12	0.0 0/12	12.5 1/8	10.0 1/10	33.3 1/3	0.0 0/5	0.0 0/2
Singapore	100.0 2/2	0.0 0/3	50.0 1/2	50.0 1/2	100.0 1/1	50.0 1/2	0.0 0/0	100.0 2/2	0.0 0/0
Sri Lanka	30.8 4/13	12.5 1/8	50.0 2/4	14.3 1/7	25.0 1/4	66.7 2/3	0.0 0/1	100.0 1/2	0.0 0/0
Commonwealth	32.6 101/310	13.1 41/312	28.2 67/238	42.5 118/278	39.4 84/213	32.9 82/249	65.3 94/144	32.2 56/174	19.7 12/61

In Asian countries some of these job categories do not exist. Few Asian universities appoint equity officers, quality assurance officers or strategic planning officers. Where these positions do exist, nearly all these jobs are held by men. India, Malaysia, Sri Lanka and Singapore are more inclined to place women into these positions than Bangladesh and Pakistan.

The pattern that emerges suggests that women are being appointed at the lecturer level but either get stuck at this level or drop out of academia, unable to combine family and academic commitments. The study concludes that "women are still severely under-represented among full-time staff in both the academic and administrative hierarchies of Commonwealth universities. Only at the level of lecturer do academic staff numbers begin to be equal but this may be a reflection as much of female drop-out and stagnation as of progress" (Lund 1998, p. 49).

Factors Disabling Women

Three perspectives explain the continuing dearth of women in senior administrative positions:

The first perspective is *person-centred* in which the paucity of women is attributed to the psycho-social attributes, including personality characteristics, attitudes and behavioural skills of women themselves. The "problem" is vested in the individual and she is called upon to adapt herself to the traditional, male concept of management within the academy. Focus is on the need for women to adapt—to compensate for their socialisation deficits. Among personal factors are lack of self esteem and self-confidence; limited aspirations in the field of management, lacking motivation and ambition to accept challenges "to go up the ladder"; women's low potential for leadership, being less assertive, less emotionally stable and lacking ability to handle a crisis (Bond 1996).

The alternative perspective, the *structure-centred* paradigm advances the view that it is the disadvantageous position of women in the organisational structure (few numbers, little power, limited access to resources) that shapes and defines the behaviour of women. The underlying premise of this perspective is that men and women are equally capable and committed to assuming positions of leadership. The "problem" is vested in the structure and the remedy is a fundamental change to eliminate inappropriate discrimination in institutional policies and practices. Among structural factors may be listed: discriminatory appointment and promotion practices; male resistance to women in management positions; absence of policies and legislation to ensure participation of women; and limited opportunities for leadership training and for demonstrating competence as a result of the power structure in the workplace (Bond 1996).

Anna Smulders explores the *culture-centred* approach "which links gender centred and organisational structure perspective". Her analysis is concerned with "the social construction of gender and the assignment of specific roles, responsibilities, and expectations to women and to men". These gender-based roles, irrelevant to the work place are carried into the workplace. She concludes that "gender relations are kept in place because the actors involved, both dominant and subordinate, subscribe to social and organisational reality" (Smulders 1998, p. 47).

Where Do Inequities Really Exist?

Little evidence can be adduced about women's inability to perform on the job. A study from India by the National Institute of Educational Planning and Administration (NIEPA) and SNDT Women's University, Bombay, of principals of women's colleges indicates that women principals function as confidently as their male counterparts.

Specific inequities lie in:

Absence of enabling conditions—access to appropriate qualifications and training (sponsorship for female academic staff for Ph.D. training), job openings; access to management structures; gender perspectives in courses; gender on the agenda for all seminars, workshops; monitoring processes to track progress; an action plan with measurable indicators of the increasing presence of women on campus. Less women participate in leadership training, are awarded overseas scholarships and get less opportunities for job related administrative training.

Discriminatory salary scales, and fringe benefits (e.g. housing or cost of living allowances) present a view that women are less suitable to be appointed to these positions. Evidence from South Africa (Budlender and Sutherland n.d.) points out that the same level of education does not bring the same return to women and men. African women earn on average between 72 and 85% of what African men earn with the same level of education. The broad conclusions reached by the Gender Pay Equity Study in Australia are: (1) as a group women staff of universities have lower levels of permanency and classification than male staff, and are more likely to be casual and part-time employees and; (2) in relation to ordinary time earnings, in universities women earned around 81% of male earnings in 1996, although the gap between male and female earnings has been diminishing over the nineties. A ground-breaking study from the Association of University Teachers (AUT), United Kingdom, *The Unequal Academy* reports that female academics working on a full-time basis earned 85% of the salary of their male colleagues in 2002–03; and male academics engaged in both teaching and research were 1.6 times more likely than their female colleagues to be counted as research active in the Research Assessment Exercise, a key determinant in promotion opportunities (AUT 2004).

Publishing productivity—A study in the United States by Creamer (1998) provides a synthesis of research on gender differences in publishing productivity. Female academics in general publish less over time than male academics. This finding is echoed in an Australian study of early career researchers (Bazeley et al. 1996, p. 32); "Males had a significantly higher total publication index than females, also for publications in which they were solo or first author". Women's performances are evaluated as less worthy and women are given fewer resources and opportunities to influence others and prove their competence, research grants, graduate students, and appointment to decision-making committees (Gardner et al. 1998).

Recruitment policies—The Unequal Academy from the United Kingdom sums up the situation well. The AUT's report shows there has been a sharp increase in the number of female academics in UK higher education, but their jobs are more casualised and less senior than those of their male colleagues. The number of female academics employed in UK higher education rose by 43% to 56,500 between 1995–96 and 2002–03. In the same period the number of male academics grew by 4% to 89,000. In all, 39% of academics are now women. But the report shows that the use of casualised fixed term contracts is far higher for women than for men. In 2002–03, 48% of women academics were employed on a fixed term contract, compared with 38% of men and that 26% of female academics now work on a part-time basis, compared with 13% of men. AUT's research also demonstrates that the glass ceiling continues to pervade university life. In almost all cases, the proportion of women on a particular academic grade decreased with the seniority of the grade. Sally Hunt, AUT's general secretary said: 'This report provides yet more evidence of the discrimination faced by women working in British universities. They are paid less, are more likely to be employed on a casual basis and continue to occupy the more junior grades'. Data from the University of Malaya indicate that women are recruited in fairly large numbers as Assistant Registrars and Financial Assistants. These positions attract a large volume of women applicants, although the university administrative service provides limited opportunities for promotion, compared with the civil service. Tendency is for men to seek employment in the more lucrative public service. There is a willingness to appoint women at that level, but greater effort made to seek applicants (usually men) for the top jobs, often from government service and public sector. Cases of long-serving female assistant registrars moving up to being registrars is not common (Asmah Haji Omar 1993).

Segregation—Some countries segregate women in schooling and exclude women from professional and administrative areas which limits opportunities for management roles for women. In such contexts women are limited in the experience they can gain of wider educational planning and can never take a central role in important decision making about education.

Cultural and structural barriers—these are the many overt and covert 'glass-ceiling' factors that impede women's career paths. These include: male managerial styles, discourse and language that 'shut' women out; informal organisational cultures also referred to as the 'old boys club'; women's reluctance to self-promote their achievements and capabilities making them institutionally 'invisible'; the persistence of cultural values and attitudes that strongly support women's childcare, family and domestic responsibilities as priority over career aspirations (Luke 1999).

'Chilly climate' for women in universities—Women often self-select out of an untenable situation of working the double-day, maintaining a competitive research and publication record, sustaining an often unreasonable teaching load, counselling and supervising students, and putting in 14 h days plus weekends in their

administrative posts (Luke 1999). Under such conditions, women's career aspirations erode, guilt mounts over the inability to 'do it all', family tensions and break-ups are not uncommon and, finally, as women pull out of the race, they confirm patriarchy's self-fulfilling prophecy that women don't have what it takes to stay the course for the long haul. This, then, makes them seem like unreliable candidates for the most highly coveted positions in the institution (Luke 1999).

The consensus appears to be that an increasing number of competent women find themselves blocked to the very top positions, and there is a feeling that subtle factors are at play preventing their crashing through the glass ceiling into the highest positions. These are filled on the basis of "trust and rapport, patronage or cloning" Reasons advanced for not appointing women may be that "it is a hard job"; "we need someone who understands the culture"; "we must have someone totally committed to the job" (Dines 1993, p. 23).

Strategies to Enhance the Contribution of Women

The literature points to a number of strategies which can impact on the status and participation of women in higher education:

Improve access to postgraduate education. The gender balance in most countries is being corrected at the undergraduate levels but there is still a paucity of women at the postgraduate levels, where a critical mass needs to be built up to seek employment in colleges and universities. Measures to overcome this situation may include making special provision for women to obtain scholarships and awards. The Commonwealth Scholarship and Fellowship Plan (CSFP) has adopted a deliberate policy to encourage countries to nominate women. Over the last 40 years of the Plan the percentage of women receiving awards has increased from 10 to 40%. Much attention also needs to be focussed on the conditions of study in Ph.D. programmes that are not women-friendly. Leonard (1997) argues strongly that recent debates in the United Kingdom about desirable form of Ph.D. ignore gender issues. Ph.D. programmes present difficulties for all those who do not fit the normal profile and they impact differently on (different groups of) men and women, who have, overall, differing family responsibilities, possibilities for geographical mobility, academic interests, etc. (pp. 152–153). That special measures which improve the conditions for post-graduate studies help women achieve a greater rate of success and completion, is well illustrated by the Council of Australian Postgraduate Associations (CAPA). CAPA's commitment to improving conditions for postgraduate women is a vital step towards improving women's participation in academia. CAPA acts as a dynamic force that ensures that the diverse category "women" are better represented in the Australian Academy. Strategies used are *lobbying*; s*upport for postgraduate studies; mentoring programmes; seminars.*

Review appointment and promotion procedures. Luke (1999) reports that lack of transparency and accountability in hiring and promotion procedures allow male managers freedom to reproduce the institution in their own image (men are more comfortable with and appoint others like them—namely other men) Sound personnel policies are therefore needed to increase number of women as academics and administrators. Universities may not have overt discriminatory procedures but neither are they likely to have transparent hiring and promotion procedures. Some affirmative action may be helpful, requiring women to be represented at all levels, especially in the key decision making committees which are responsible for establishing promotion criteria, selecting conference representatives, allocation of funds, research awards and support facilities within universities. Information on all aspects of promotion criteria should be widely known. Absence from the key committees, leaves important information to remain largely in the 'old boys' network.

Provide special programmes for women. The need for special awareness and training programmes is widely recognised. Such programmes have been introduced by institutions, by development agencies and by associations of universities and colleges. These usually encompass a wide range of activities. Two examples will suffice: (1) The new Mainstreaming Scheme of Monash University which comprises a range of strategies aimed at effecting organisational and thereby cultural change. These strategies include: a Vice-Chancellor's Taskforce for the Advancement of Women, which advises on organisational change strategies such as equity targets, policy directions etc.; a Senior Women's Forum which meets regularly to discuss various issues such as strategic directions, research possibilities, networking etc.; support to various university mentoring schemes;. special assistance to women looking to be promoted; responding to individual queries by matching up interested women with developmental opportunities at the university; organising functions such as International Women's Day, breakfasts etc.; regular communications through the internal staff newsletter, including profiling a woman staff member each fortnight; and a website to inform staff about the Scheme. (2) The Association of Commonwealth Universities' Women's Programme which at a pan-Commonwealth level includes sensitising and training workshops, production of training materials, training of trainers, electronic networking, monitoring progress of women, promoting exchange schemes, lobbying and advocacy, promotion of formal courses, encouraging gender management, presenting a regular feature on the programme in the *ACU Bulletin*, and maintaining a website for members.

Provide legislative and infrastructure support. Special programmes for women are necessary but they should be backed at government and institutional level by anti-discrimination legislation and regulation. The provision of legislative and infrastructure support is a tangible expression of organisational recognition and undoubtedly can make a great difference to the capacity of women to manage multiple roles. To overcome prolonged deprivation, the 1986 National Education Policy in India accorded women the privileges of free education and reservation in educational institutions. The national education system was expected to play a positive, interventionist role in the empowerment of women with a "well conceived edge in favour of women". The objectives by 2000 was to enroll in various professional degree courses so as to increase their number in medicine, teaching, engineering and other fields substantially (Joshi 1999). In Australia, two pieces of legislation were enacted: 1984 *Sex Discrimination Act.*, and the 1986 *Affirmative Action (Equal Employment Opportunity for Women) Act.* The provision include the requirement of employers with 100 or more employees to develop an affirmative action program and to report annually on this program to the Affirmative Action Agency. The legislation outlines four areas for review: recruitment and selection, promotion and transfer, training and development and conditions of employment (Spoor and Lewis 1997).

Change the rules, then the attitudes. Firm in the belief that if you change the rules, then attitudes will change, a number of institutions and organisations have moved to change the rules governing all aspects of management. The Commonwealth Secretariat is an example of an international organisation which, to ensure adequate women's participation, has tried to institute rules regarding project development, participation in workshops, representation on committees etc. At the international level it has proposed the Commonwealth Plan of Action for Gender and Development. These initiatives have run concurrent with an intensive pro-gramme of gender sensitisation for all its officers. An institutional example comes from the University of the South Pacific whose Network of Women in Higher Education in the Pacific (NetWHEP) formulated a Women's Charter and took it through the university senate as an official policy document to govern all aspects of university administration. This represents a major initiative by the Pacific women and a landmark charter to ensure gender equity in higher education in the Pacific.

Institute gender equity policies. In the west, equity units and policies are institutionalised in most universities. Provisions include equity targets (e.g., com-mittee representation; hiring, promotion, and tenure targets, etc.); policies for the non-sexist use of language in University documents; provision of mentoring and management training programs; workplace childcare; career management, retire-ment or investment seminars; annual accountability to federal agencies on hiring, tenure, and promotions benchmarks and targets (Luke). A recent example comes from Australia where the Australian Vice-Chancellor's Committee has adopted a five-year Action Plan setting out the policies, targets and time frames for Australian higher education to achieve better gender equity.

Engender university management. All the strategies advocated above may be achieved by higher education institutions by incorporating an overall Gender Management System (GMS). Institutions truly need to be engendered in all aspects of their management to provide women with an enabling environment in which they are not penalised for the multi-faceted roles they perform. A lesson maybe taken from the experience of Makerere University in Uganda which has recently launched a programme to engender all aspects of its management. The overall objective of this Gender Management System (GMS) is to ensure gender sensitivity in the governance and administration of Makerere University, so that its delivery of services to its stakeholders—students, staff and the wider society—can lead to sustainable human development in Uganda, with men and women sharing responsibilities and enjoying the benefits equitably. The process has analysed the issues that have given rise to concerns about gender inequality in university governance, management and administration; explored women-specific issues in diagnosing gender inequality at Makerere; developed an appropriate action plan for a gender management system to support the mainstreaming of gender at Makerere. Future action will include: integration of gender into university curriculum and research; incorporation of gender into instructional methods and techniques; establishment and/or strengthening of gender-sensitive policies with regard to admission to and for the administration and academic management of the university; encouragement and establishment of gender-inclusive extra-curricular activities; specific provision for social and career guidance to ensure that women students and staff are fully integrated in the university.

Outcomes of Leadership Programmes for Women

The evidence from evaluation reports of women in leadership programmes is that they can play an important role in promoting gender equity.

An Australian Technology Network Women's Executive Development Programme (ATN WEXDEV) evaluation reported that leadership programmes benefited both individual women and the institutions they worked for. As a result of their programmes:

Women participants were seen to have

- developed enhanced skills that enabled them to undertake leadership positions;
- re-valued their own skills;
- formulated viable career goals;
- developed understanding of leadership concepts;
- increased their organisational management knowledge;
- increased their understanding of the cultures of universities;
- strengthened networking opportunities and
- found greater access to promotions or professional advancement.

The encouragement of women as leaders and senior executives was also seen to have benefits for universities:

- increased numbers and proportions of women in leadership positions;
- development of a culture more inclusive of diversity;
- improved quality of university leadership and
- more representative decision-making.

Evaluation of *Leadership Development for Women (LDW)* of the University of Western Australia, carried out by de Vries, measures quantifiable changes that have occurred in the participants' working lives that can be attributed to their involvement in the programme. It reported on the following aspects:

- *Promotion*—LDW participants are more successful in achieving promotion than all other staff groups, including non-LDW women and men. 47% of the 1994 LDW academic participants were successful in achieving promotion compared with 12% of the non-LDW female academic group, 15% of the male academic group and a total promotion rate of 15%. 22% of the 1995 LDW academic participants were successful in achieving promotion compared with 8% of the non-LDW female group, 10% of the male academic group and a total promotion rate of 10%. 10% of the 1996 LDW academic participants were successful in achieving promotion compared with 3% of the non-LDW female group, 5% of the male academic group and a total promotion rate of 5%. The survey revealed that 77% of those who had applied for promotion were successful in achieving promotion, 59% felt their decision to apply for promotion was influenced by LDW and 82% felt the quality of their application was influenced by participation in the program.
- *Retention Rates* are higher for all LDW groups in comparison to non-LDW women and men. Retention rates for LDW women vary between 89 and 95% compared to 57–88% for other groups.
- *Changes in working life*—the most frequently noted changes for participants: Participation in UWA networks; becoming more visible at UWA; being offered or applying for new projects; and becoming involved in women's networks. Also increased confidence, feel more valued, willing to take greater challenges, better organised, becoming a mentor, the quality of their applications for promotion.
- *Conclusion*—LDW participants are clearly faring better in the University system than women who have not been part of the programme. They are much more likely to be promoted and more likely to remain employed in UWA. They self-report significant changes in their working lives they attribute to their programme involvement. As a result the University has more women in more senior positions contributing to decision making. Crucial outcome for the university as it seeks to attract and retain the best staff and to redress its gender balance.

The **AVCC** recently announced that in 1996, there were 2 female Vice-Chancellors (5%); in 2003—10 (27%). Over a similar time-span, in 1996 there were 19 women in DVC, PVC and Dean positions (19%); in 2003 there were 27 (21%). The number and proportion of women in senior administrative posts (Directors) were 230 women in 1996 (26%) and 423 in 2003 (36%).

In a recent study (yet unpublished) conducted by Colleen Chesterman and colleagues for ATN WEXDEV in Australia the key research question was whether a significant proportion of women in senior positions changed the dominant cultures in institutions. Almost all interviewees, men and women, spoke of the ways in which women encouraged collaboration and consultation, built consensus and teamwork, were innovative and approachable and focused attention on fellow staff and students. These were often identified with female management styles, but have become generalised as acceptable contemporary management techniques.

Conclusion

The proportion of women enrolled in tertiary education institutions and in key decision-making positions in nearly all Commonwealth countries still falls short of the 53% that would represent female population, and falls short even of the 30% endorsed by Commonwealth Heads of Government and by the UN Economic and Social Council. Clearly, there is need for sustained efforts to further enhance women's status in higher education.

To conclude, women are "eminently capable researchers and scholars, intellectuals, administrators, managers, and leaders. But they are also the social and emotional glue of any society: childbearers, childrearers, carers of kin and the aged." Despite their extraordinary abilities, and "pivotal role" in society, they are consistently undervalued and "their aspirations thwarted". Society is impoverished if they are denied "the structural and ideological support that would enable their full and equal access, participation, and share of reward outcomes in the professions of their choice".... "Women need to take charge of their educational goals and professional aspirations" (Luke 1999).

References

Asmah Haji Omar, (1993). Women managers in higher education in Malaysia. In E. Dines (Ed.), *Women in higher education management* (pp. 123–136). Paris, France: UNESCO/Commonwealth Secretariat.

Association of University Teachers (AUT). (2004). *The unequal academy.* London, England: Association of University Teachers.

Bazeley, P., et al. (1996). *Waiting in the wings: A study of early career researchers in Australia.* Canberra, Australia: Australian Government Publishing Service.

Bond, S. (1996). *Academic leadership (Unpublished trainers module).* London, England: Commonwealth Secretariat.

Budlender, D., & Sutherland, C. (n.d.). *National score card. Country: South Africa.* Forum for African Women Educationalists, South Africa (FAWESA).

Creamer, E. (1998). *Assessing faculty publication productivity: Issues of equity.* ASHE-ERIC Higher Education Report Volume 26, No 2. Washington, DC: The George Washington University.

Dines, E. (Ed.). (1993). *Women in higher education management.* Paris, France: UNESCO/ Commonwealth Secretariat.

Gardner, M., Edwards, A., & Ramsey, E. (1998). *Women in Australian universities: Findings from recent research and policy implications.* Paper presented at the 1998 Australian Vice-Chancellors Committee Retreat.

Joshi, S. (1999). *Empowerment of women administrators in educational organisations.* Unpublished paper, Faculty of Education and Psychology, the M.S. University of Baroda, India.

Leonard, D. (1997). Gender issues in doctoral studies. In N. Graves & V. Verma (Eds.), *Working for a doctorate: A guide for the humanities and the social sciences* (pp. 152–183). New York, NY: Routledge.

Luke, C. (1999). Women's career mobility in higher education: Case studies in South-East Asia. *ACU Bulletin of Current Documentation, 139,* 18–20.

Lund, H. (1998). *A single sex profession? Female staff numbers in Commonwealth Universities*. London, England: The Commonwealth Higher Education Management Service.

Singh, J. K. S. (2002a). *Women and management in higher education management: A good practice handbook*. Paris, France: UNESCO.

Singh, J. K. S. (2002b). *Still a single sex profession? Female staff numbers in Commonwealth Universities*. London, England: Association of Commonwealth Universities Gender Equity Programme.

Smulders, A. E. M. (1998). *Creating space for women: Gender linked factors in managing staff in higher education institutions*. Paris, France: UNESCO, International Institute for Educational Planning.

Spoor, E., & Lewis, C. (1997). Gender imbalance in higher education: The Australian experience. In F. Gale & B. Goldflam (Eds.), *Strategies to redress gender imbalance in numbers of senior academic women* (pp. 34–47). Perth: University of Western Australia.

Author Biography

Professor Jasbir Kaur Ph.D., B.Ed. (postgraduate), B.A. Hons. (Malaya) is a former Professor of Sociological Studies, Faculty of Education, University of Malaya; Dean, Institute of Advanced Studies, University of Malaya and Chief Programme Officer (Higher Education Co-operation), Commonwealth Secretariat, London, UK. Her time at the Commonwealth Secretariat opened new opportunities to work in the area of development process for higher education in Commonwealth countries. She was closely associated with the development and implementation of a women in higher education programme designed to enhance the participation of women in the leadership and management of higher education and a programme for student exchange among Commonwealth universities known as the Commonwealth Study Abroad Consortium (CUSAC). Professor Jasbir has undertaken major evaluation studies and surveys for international agencies such as the World Bank, UNESCO, and Commonwealth Secretariat, the Association of Commonwealth Universities and the International Labour Organisation. Her principal areas of research and publication are education and social occupational mobility, assess and equity in education, women leadership and management in higher education, student learning orientation and education and national development. She has continued her work with women in higher education leadership and management as Consultant to the Association of Commonwealth Universities' Gender Programme for which she has prepared reports on the status of women in Commonwealth universities, assisted in training workshops for academic women in many Commonwealth countries in Africa, the Indian sub-continent, the Carribean and the United Kingdom, and prepared a good practice handbook for women in leadership and management in higher education.

Chapter 10
Motivation, Engagement, and Educational Performance: International Perspectives

Julian Elliott

Synopsis

(Compiled from slide presentation)

Dr. Ruth Wong was a true internationalist who, during her long career, developed a global perspective on the interaction between education and larger social and economic systems. She recognised the importance of traditional values, the need to embrace new and creative ideas and the powerful effect of social changes upon educational outcomes. Such an understanding closely reflects themes that underpin this lecture.

The first part of the presentation discussed a five-year cross-cultural study of achievement motivation in children in England, the USA and Russia involving surveys of more than 6000 students and 3000 parents, detailed interviews with students and teachers, and a series of field observations. Secondly, the lecture discussed the impact of recent socio-economic and socio-political upheaval upon achievement motivation in Russian schools. Questions were raised about the ability of current achievement motivation theory (in particular, attribution theory and goal theory) and methodology, to provide rich and meaningful understandings about those factors that lead individuals, communities, cultures and nations to commit to academic study.

The implications of these studies and lessons to be learnt were deliberated. As Dr. Wong wrote 30 years ago, "Education is largely an enterprise launched in faith: the gestation period before results are seen is long" (Wong 1976, p. 19).

J. Elliott (✉)
Collingwood College, Durham University, South Road, Durham DH1 3LT, UK
e-mail: joe.elliott@dur.ac.uk

© Springer Nature Singapore Pte Ltd. 2017   119
O.S. Tan et al. (eds.), *Global Voices in Education*,
DOI 10.1007/978-981-10-3539-5_10

Much of the material covered in his presentation is drawn from a series of journal studies that has been synthesised to produce his co-authored book *Motivation, Engagement and Educational Performance*, published by Palgrave Macmillan (Elliott et al. 2005).

Source: National Institute of Education (Singapore) News.

References

Elliott, J. G., Hufton, N. R., Willis, W., & Illushin, L. (2005). *Motivation, engagement and educational performance: International perspectives on the contexts for learning*. New York, NY: Palgrave Macmillan.

Wong, R. (1976). Education in Singapore: National and international perspectives. *Final report: Education of our youth for today's changing world* (pp. 16–22). Singapore: Ministry of Education.

Author Biography

Professor Julian (Joe) Elliott is an academic and educational psychologist. He is currently Professor of Education and Principal of Collingwood College at the University of Durham. Prof. Elliott qualified as a teacher in mainstream and special schools. He subsequently practiced as an educational psychologist before entering higher education in 1990, first as a lecturer and in 1998 he became a professor with the award of a personal chair within the School of Education. After fourteen years at the University of Sunderland where he became Acting Dean of the university's School of Education and Lifelong Learning, he returned to Durham in 2004. His research interests include behavior management, achievement motivation, dynamic assessment, cognitive education and special education. He is the Immediate Past President of the International Association for Cognitive Education and Psychology. In addition to his university work, he sits on a number of editorial boards. He is the Associate Editor of the British Journal of Educational Psychology and he is a member of the board for the British Educational Research Journal Learning and Individual Differences, and Comparative Education.

He has authored and co-authored many books and published many articles. A recent book he co-authored with Elena L. Grigorenko titled *The Dyslexia Debate* was published in early 2014.

Appendix

List of Memorial Lectures and Speakers (1983–2008)

Year	Speaker	Title
1983	Robert Dreeben	Some thoughts about teaching and learning
1984	Hugh W.S. Philp	The concept of educational disadvantage and some implications for the classroom teacher
1985	Marie M. Clay	Beginning literacy in two languages
1986	Cho-Yee To	Utilization of new knowledge and application of new ideas in education: A discussion of the vitalization of education as a profession and discipline
1987	Malcolm Skilbeck	Education and the changing economic and industrial order: An international perspective
1988	William Taylor	Research and the improvement of teaching
1989	Ungku Abdul Aziz	A vision of education in the 21st century
1990	Lucrecia R. Kasilag	Music education for national development: The Philippine experience
1991	Neville Bennett	Recent conceptions of children's learning: Implications for classroom practice
1992	Barry McGaw	Measuring and monitoring educational achievement
1993	Lilian G. Katz	Engaging children's minds: innovative research and practice
1994	Wong Kooi Sim	A personal philosophy of education
1995	Richard A. Pring	The professional education of teachers
1996	Gungwu Wang	National education and the scientific tradition
1997	Awang Had Salleh	Approaching the new millennium: Education at the crossroads
1998	Warwick Elley	Breaking the cycle of literacy disadvantage in the 21st century
1999	Paul Min Phang Chang	Educational administration: New challenges and responses

(continued)

© Springer Nature Singapore Pte Ltd. 2017
O.S. Tan et al. (eds.), *Global Voices in Education*,
DOI 10.1007/978-981-10-3539-5

(continued)

Year	Speaker	Title
2000	Hon Chan Chai	Education and human resources development for the knowledge economy: A personal perspective
2001	Angus M. Gunn	The timeless teacher: Contemporary research and ancient models
2002	No lecture	
2003	No lecture	
2004	Jasbir Kaur	Women and leadership in institutions of higher learning
2005	Courtney B. Cazden	The value of principled eclecticism in education reform: 1965–2005
2006	Julian Elliott	Motivation, engagement and educational performance: International perspectives
2007	Elena L. Grigorenko	Schooling today: Teaching competence, creativity and compassion
2008	David Tzuriel	Mediated learning experience (MLE) strategies and children's cognitive plasticity

Index

© Springer Nature Singapore Pte Ltd. 2017
O.S. Tan et al. (eds.), *Global Voices in Education*,
DOI 10.1007/978-981-10-3539-5